"Mike Sares is a hero to me as I have watched his missional heart over many years and his dedication to Jesus and the gospel. Reading the pages of *Pure Scum* is like reading a continuing chapter in the book of Acts. It is an adventurous, risk-taking, inspiring, unusual, mission-focused story about people who are passionate about those who are often missed by the average church. You will be encouraged and thrilled through these pages, and your heart will grow in love for those whom Jesus loves."

DAN KIMBALL, author of *They Like Jesus but Not the Church*

"Reading *Pure Scum* inspired me to love more when it's not convenient or easy, to embrace the risk-taking that inherently comes with following Jesus. What a messy, beautiful, hard-knocks and sovereign story of how God continues to use crews of misfits to share who he is with the world."

AMENA BROWN, poet, journalist, speaker

"Mike Sares has written a book with a huge heart and a deep soul. Harrowing at times, brutally honest, filled with love for the people and neighborhood he pastors, *Pure Scum* is Mike's exploration of his journey following Christ—into places few people would willingly go. That Mike goes there joyfully (and painfully) is an amazing thing to behold. That we get to follow along behind him as he does is an opportunity that should not be missed."

TIM KEEL, author of *Intuitive Leadership*

"Truly a moving portrait of the Father's love in our present time. A love for the undesirable and down___ ___dden of this world, sheep and shepherds alike. Mike h__ ___ ___ _____ Good Shepherd's example and by his grace feed_ ___ ___ ___ __ _e and humility."

D___   Wovenhand, 16 Horsepower

"M___ ___ ___ ___ __an write an inspiring book: he has lived an i__ ___ ___vo to Sares and Scum of the Earth Church for daring to love the goths, the punks, the skaters, the rag-taggers who resemble Jesus' posse far better than the scrubbed-up, respectable façades we parade on Sundays. Sares offers wise counsel and a biblical foundation along with these moving stories. This is a must-read for anyone who dreams of reaching the fringes, the right-brained and the left-out with God's amazing grace."

SUSAN E. ISAACS, author of *Angry Conversations with God*

"Stunning! Søren Kierkegaard writes: 'My complaint is not that this age is wicked but that it is paltry. It lacks passion.' Scum has the passion that we lack in the church. Nehemiah 11 records the request to go back to the city. Scum never left; we did. It is time to go back, and this book leads the way."

RICH HURST, pastor of leadership and staff development, McLean Bible Church

"The unlikely story, of an unlikely pastor, leading an unlikely church, with an unlikely name. But the evidence of God's grace fills every chapter, and it is sure to inspire many who long to see Christ in the unlikely corners of our world."

SKYE JETHANI, author of *The Divine Commodity*

"This is not a book! Rather *Pure Scum* is a conversation about Jesus and his church that most of us need to have over a bottomless Sumatra. Like all stories of Christians living on the edge, this one is funny and sad, inspiring and disagreeable, and appealing and revolting. Always interesting and always biblical, you will have coffee with Mike again and again as you realize, 'Shifting to follow Jesus in a new direction is not always greeted with applause.'"

DAVE CARDER, author of *Torn Asunder* and *Close Calls*

"Mike Sares boldly colors outside the lines of creativity, innovation and necessity, challenging all of us to reconsider what the church looks like and what it's meant to be. After all, what other church in America dubs their smokers the greeting team? *Pure Scum* is a story of radical grace— one we all need to experience and embrace."

MARGARET FEINBERG, author of *The Organic God* and *Scouting the Divine*

"Mike Sares and his friends at Scum of the Earth Church have been on the ride of their lives—and thanks to *Pure Scum* we get to ride shot-gun! Come for the stories, stay for the theological, pastoral and leadership insights."

DON EVERTS, minister of outreach, Bonhomme Presbyterian Church, St. Louis

"Not simply a biography, not simply a glimpse of modern church history, in chapter after chapter Mike Sares tells bits of his own story to reveal how God used every step of his journey to shape him into the pastor of a church called Scum of the Earth. With incredible humility, Mike neither hides nor flaunts his failings but constantly points to the grace of God, a trait truly characteristic of his life as a pastor. The stories of the people he's pastored are both heartbreaking and life-giving, a testimony always to God's work amongst the least and the lost, the beautiful and the painful that make up the congregation of Scum. All in all, this book is a testimony to the pastor that Mike is, the unusual church that Scum is, and, more than anything, the work that God can do when his people let go and listen."

MARIAM KAMELL, coauthor of *James* (Zondervan Exegetical Commentary on the New Testament)

"Great explorers don't observe from the safety of the ship. They grab a skiff, go on shore, meet the natives, take measurements and make a map. In his book Mike Sares provides a map for us, with rich details about what life looks like in the land of humility, honesty and brokenness. He introduces us to the King of that land—the Lord Jesus—and makes us want to move there permanently (even though it lacks many conveniences of the place we call home). Mike's chapter on love is worth the price of the whole book. Oh, and unlike most books that tell you everything they know in the first three chapters and then fill in the rest with meaningless stuff, Mike's book just gets better and better as you close in on the end. You might actually think about starting with the final chapter and reading your way back to the front."

JIM HENDERSON, author of *Jim and Casper Go to Church*

Pure Scum

The Left-Out, the Right-Brained
and the Grace of God

Mike Sares

Foreword by
Reese Roper,
Five Iron Frenzy

IVP Books

An imprint of InterVarsity Press
Downers Grove, Illinois

InterVarsity Press
P.O. Box 1400, Downers Grove, IL 60515-1426
World Wide Web: www.ivpress.com
E-mail: email@ivpress.com

InterVarsity Press® is the book-publishing division of InterVarsity Christian Fellowship/USA®, a movement of students and faculty active on campus at hundreds of universities, colleges and schools of nursing in the United States of America, and a member movement of the International Fellowship of Evangelical Students. For information about local and regional activities, write Public Relations Dept., InterVarsity Christian Fellowship/USA, 6400 Schroeder Rd., P.O. Box 7895, Madison, WI 53707-7895, or visit the IVCF website at <www.intervarsity.org>.

Design: Jonathan Till
Images: Rural school children in Texas, 1943. John Vachon/Library of Congress, LC-USW36-830

ISBN 978-0-8308-3629-1

Printed in the United States of America ∞

Library of Congress Cataloging-in-Publication Data

Sares, Mike, 1954-
    Pure Scum: the left-out, the right-brained, and the grace of God /
Mike Sares.
        p. cm.
    ISBN 978-0-8308-3629-1 (pbk.: alk. paper)
    1. Scum of the Earth Church (Denver, Colo.) 2. Sares, Mike, 1954-
I. Title.
    BX9999.D467S27 2010
    289.9'50978883—dc22

                                                                2009048956

P	21	20	19	18	17	16	15	14	13	12	11	10	9	8	7	6	5	4	3	2	1
Y	27	26	25	24	23	22	21	20	19	18	17	16	15	14	13	12	11	10			

Dedication

For Mary Patricia Francel Sares

Miluji tĕ. Σ´ αγαπώ. I love you.

Contents

Acknowledgments

$\mathcal{M}$argaret Feinberg and Leif Oines, I am in your loving debt. You put me together with the Likewise Books folks. You helped me to start and finish this book in your home (and even took dictation when I was stuck). You kept me focused and pushed me to be a better writer. Thanks gobs and gobs and gobs.

David Zimmerman, you're a superhero without the cape or tights. (Hmm . . . I probably shouldn't have mentioned tights. An editor would have deleted that reference, I'll bet.) Your vision for Likewise and this project, and your masterful editing, made this book much better than it would have been.

Big thanks to Anna Till and Mollie Fitzpatrick for help in typing the manuscript from stuff I said. Good thing they deleted my ridiculously long pauses.

Thanks to Chad Allen of Baker Books for helping me gather my thoughts in a cohesive outline and for the pithy chapter titles. (And thanks for not hating me for going with Likewise. My only defense is from Acts 26:19: "So then, *Chad*, I was not disobedient to the vision from heaven.")

Joy and Scotty Sawyer, you were the first to envision this book back when Scum of the Earth began. Joy told me that being fired earlier was "God's kiss on my forehead." (Smartypants.)

"The Preaching Team"—Rev. Les Avery, Rev. Jim Emig and

Rev. Steve Garcia—your wisdom is peppered throughout *Pure Scum*. Without you, much of my life would suck swamp water. I'm not talking about the beverage. I'm talking about the stuff that sustains mosquito larvae.

And here's to Ray Nethery, Ned Berube and the Alliance for Renewal Churches (a.k.a. "The Rebel Alliance"). You took me in when others balked at the idea. You're like my own Obi-Wan and Yoda. You make 1 Thessalonians 5:11-13 an easy task.

Jonathan Till, Scum's Designer Laureate: you've known that I've always been an unstylish guy stuck in the middle of much hipper people. Thanks for making the *book* look cool, at least.

Books take time. I so appreciate the council and staff at Scum of the Earth Church, who granted me a sabbatical, filled in during my absences and put up with my necessity to focus on writing at times. We're in this story together, so, uh, let's make it . . . um . . . a comedy!

Special thanks to my wife, Mary, who helped me to remember the things I forgot, and to correct things I remembered. You could've stopped the whole Scum thing from happening in the first place; thanks for taking the risk with me! Thanks to our children, Katina, Sophia, Luke and Ethan, who in ways that few understand took that risk without having a choice to do so or not.

And thanks to Mom and Dad for telling me to finally go to Denver Seminary.

Δεῦτε προσκυνήσωμεν καὶ προσπέσωμεν Χριστῷ. Σῶσον ἡμᾶς, Υἱὲ Θεοῦ ὁ ἀναστὰς ἐκ νεκρῶν, ψάλλοντάς σοι· Ἀλληλούϊα.

Invocation

$\mathcal{A}$t the funerals of ancient Greek warriors, it was simple. No one wasted the time and effort we spend in the modern era trying to justify the lives of the deceased by assigning meaning to their deaths, or attempting to grasp something purposeful in their lives that we may apply to our own. Instead, only one question was asked of the recently departed by the friends and family that gathered to remember them: "Did they live with passion?" Mike Sares is, without any argument, the most passionate person I have ever met.

In the summer of 1995 I was a very lost young college student who had stumbled through the doors of the church nearest to my house. I had recently been asked to leave the third church I had been to in four years—either that or cut my hair, or at least stop dying it obnoxiously bright colors, and get rid of some of the earrings and the nose ring. It was, in a way, the death of church as I knew it. Not that I had stopped believing in Christ or that the church had ceased to be alive to me, but that the smaller institution of church—as in "the building"—was becoming far less relevant to me. And as it quietly started to slip away, and as I was somehow attempting to find purpose and meaning in that death (much in the same way we still do at funerals), I met Mike.

He was, at the time, the young adults director at Corona Presbyterian Church in the Capitol Hill neighborhood of Denver. I had gone there expecting to be shunned, or at least looked down on, but that was never the case. Every person I met there genuinely accepted me for who I was. Something beyond the superficiality of handshakes and "turning to the people next to you and greeting them" existed there, and at its apex was Michael Sares.

In the beginning, three or four of us from Five Iron Frenzy were going there, because, as I said, it was the closest church to our house. What transpired was an act of what I can only say with tremendous understatement—providence. Where others saw rebellion, Mike could somehow only see potential. When he found out that there was some sort of "punk band with horns" attending his church, instead of condemning us, he steered another of his parishioners, Dennis Culp, to try out as our trombonist. Not only did Dennis become the musical anchor of our band, but soon Mike became our spiritual mainstay. He pursued us all vigilantly, sometimes helping us to sift through record contracts, sometimes feeding us, sometimes providing advice and, oftentimes, just listening.

Mike is a natural shepherd, and were it not for all of the botched attempts at mentoring inflicted on me throughout my formative years, I would never have known what a great mentor Mike really is. Over the past thirteen years that I have known him, he has been a pastor, a friend and a father figure to me. This book is about that—not just a story about mentoring but a story of how Mike saw the value of just taking in some lost punk-rocker-type college kids, and believing in them.

In February 2000, Mike and I took his natural ability as a shepherd and our pseudo-fame as a band, and created a very small church out of it. No one could have guessed that it would have gone this far. Scum of the Earth has been touted as "the church for the left-out and the right-brained," and it has become a far larger movement than any of us ever hoped. What I wish for, as you read this book, is that you will see the value of mentoring and, most important, of seeking out the lost and underestimated in our society. It is my hope that the notion of the grace of God extended to the left-out and the right-brained will seep through these pages, and that it will haunt you, pervading your own lives and vocations . . . as it still does mine.

Godspeed,
Reese Roper

1

To Refuse or Not to Refuse

Up to this moment we have become the scum of the earth, the refuse of the world.

*I*t's just church. I have never seen it as anything unusual. As one of the staff members at Scum of the Earth says, "It's not that we're doing church differently—we're just doing church with different people." The trademarked advice I offer to visitors to a service is simply, "Keep your expectations low, and you'll be happy."

We sing a lot of the same songs at Scum as other churches. A sermon series usually takes us through a book of the Bible. We serve communion just like churches have done for a couple of millennia now. We don't have a mosh pit, a smoke machine or a light show. But this is the group of people with whom I have been placed, and it's the backdrop of my story. This is a place where everyone is welcome, a place that we like to call "the church for the left-out and the right-brained."

People ask me all the time why I would allow a church to be called Scum of the Earth. They assume that, like most young churches, we just tried to make our name as cool as possible. But Scum of the Earth is a name that is humble. It's also biblical. When the apostle Paul was describing the way the world treated him and the other apostles who were doing their best to follow Christ, he used the name of our church: "we have become the scum of the earth, the refuse of the world" (1 Cor 4:9-13).

Scum is an appropriate name for a church trying to connect with people who have been outcast by the rest of society or by churches. Many can identify with the name Scum because they've endured this type of treatment before. The name also serves as a reminder of our need for God and redemption. In addition, it's just plain funny.

I was not in favor of the name at first. But I have come to believe that it was one of the best things that could have happened to us. Amazing things began happening right away as the Lord brought people around our fledgling church.

One of the first women to come to Scum of the Earth went by the name "Friday" because she looked like Wednesday from *The Addams Family*. Normally she wore black nail polish, black clothes, whitish make-up and dyed-black hair with purple bangs. She was a waitress at an all-night restaurant our group would go to after Bible study on Monday nights. She didn't grow up with any religious background, but the way people at Scum loved her drew her relentlessly to Jesus. One night, after watching a movie with a few others, she got a call at home from one of the girls from the church. Melanie was crying for Friday; she felt deeply that God wanted to touch her life. Friday thought Melanie was "being an emotional girl," but it got her thinking about the new friends she had made and their faith in Jesus.

A few days later, after thinking about it for some time, Friday decided to ask God to make himself real to her, too. She didn't know whether to "wish it, or say it, or pray it," since she had never done anything like that before. After praying she began having dreams of someone who reminded her vaguely of her father.

He was speaking to her in the middle of all the bad things she had done and been a part of, asking, "Is this the way you want the rest of your life to be?"

"No, this isn't what I want," she replied.

He said, "Then just believe."

I didn't have much to do with Friday's experience, beyond helping her put words to what God was already doing in her heart. I felt like a little boy whose dad asked him to help fix the washing machine; I was holding the flashlight while he did all the repairs. God was at work in our small, humble community, and I had the pleasure of watching.

Even though I'm the pastor, my experience at Scum of the Earth is really not that different from Friday's. I had a dream in those early days as well.

My wife, Mary, and I were on the campus of some old university. There was a large old building with a dome. The doors and the shutters were closed, but the entire building was bulging and pulsing. A tremendous amount of water was building up on the inside. Suddenly the building burst open with a huge stream of water gushing forth from it. It looked like there would be no end to the water pouring out. I told Mary that we needed to run to higher ground and see what was going to happen.

When we got to the top of the hill, we looked down and saw young men and women riding the waves of that stream—surfboarding, body surfing, swimming in the clear sparkling water, jumping in, being delightfully swept along by the current. There were also large flat rafts with people on them floating down this new river. The rafts were behind the initial surge of water (where it was a bit more calm) picking up tired swimmers. They would lie in the warm sun as the raft went down the stream.

This whole scene was marked by an atmosphere of great fun, and frolicking, and adventure, and risk, and excitement. We felt privileged to be watching. After I woke up, I remember asking the Lord what the dream might mean. The thought came to my mind that we would definitely enjoy watching what his Spirit was going to do in the days ahead.

God is at work today, same as he has always been, preparing the hearts and minds of young people all over the world for the ride of their lives—if they will only give themselves to Jesus. Nothing could be more inspiring, invigorating and fulfilling. It is my hope that this book not only encourages people to dive in but also prompts others to take care of those who have.

Diving in is fun, but it's also dangerous. There are rapids downstream—large boulders upon which we could be crushed. There are downed trees blocking the way and dangerous, swirling pools where the current can suck a person down. Diving into a life of following Jesus led all but one of his disciples to be executed, but other people have suffered different dangers: they've been rejected by friends or family, they've lost jobs and other opportunities, they've had their whole understanding of what's important turned upside down. They have changed countries and occupations, learned new languages and customs, given up material goods and fortunes.

Why would these followers of Jesus, from the first to the most recent, risk so much to follow him? I think part of the answer is that they couldn't refuse the exhilarating adventure of a life following Christ in a community that understands them and the risk they've entered into. The great irony is that it looked to so many like they threw their lives away, becoming the scum of the earth. Those of us who are scum know better.

2

𝕾𝖈𝖚𝖒

Vision, Passion & Suffering

*For it seems to me that God has put us
apostles on display at the end of the procession,
like men condemned to die in the arena.*

I grew up Greek Orthodox. Very Greek Orthodox. All four of my grandparents were Greek immigrants, so in addition to attending Sunday school and a liturgical church service every week sung and spoken in a language I was only mildly interested in understanding, I went to Greek school twice a week in the evenings. There was a common truth for kids growing up like me: try as we might to the contrary, we knew that we were different.

My mom died when I was twelve, and I became a kid striving for acceptance. I did everything at school, it seemed—sports, student government, band and various clubs—but inside I still always felt a bit outside of my friends' inner circle. Perhaps it was because I wouldn't go drinking with them; that's where a lot of their bonding took place. I was afraid to get drunk with them because I thought that if I let my guard down, they'd see me for who I really was and I'd be teased or totally excluded. This is a common feeling among young people, but back then I just kept it bottled up. Even though everyone knew me, I don't think anybody knew me well.

In my junior year I got to know some Christian kids, primarily because one of the girls in the group paid some attention to me. The fact that she was pretty somehow made her views about religion interesting. (I'm not proud of this fact. But in my own defense, I was only seventeen.) A buddy of hers and then her youth pastor did their best to introduce me to Jesus. I even prayed a prayer of salvation with the youth pastor, but the truth was that I just didn't get it. Soon, however, things would change for me in a big way.

My dad remarried an "American woman," as the Greeks in my church called her. They even called it a "mixed marriage." We moved to a new house in another school district and began attending a Presbyterian church one week and a Greek Orthodox Church the next. That rocked my world. I had never sung from a hymnbook before, never had communion from a tiny plastic cup with a cracker, never heard a choir sing in English, never even knew bell choirs existed, and never had *not* done the sign of the cross a few dozen times during a church service. I could go on, but I won't.

I transferred to a new high school two weeks into my senior year. At my old school I had been class president; here I walked the halls day by day as nothing more than the new kid. To my adolescent surprise, nobody at my new school really cared about student government. Immediately stripped of friendships with the "cool and smart" people, I realized the shaky ground upon which I had built my small amount of confidence.

I did make some new friends, and I met several kids who attended a Christian outreach to high school students. The Young Life meetings would take place in different people's basements. They would sing songs about Jesus, with lyrics such as "He's Everything to Me," and then this college guy would stand up and talk for about fifteen minutes. The talk was interesting, but I felt like I was lying every time I sang. So I left.

I had to settle the Jesus question once and for all; I wanted to start drinking in earnest and begin satisfying my sexual curiosity with impunity. So I began checking out a group that now, in retrospect, I can only describe as a cult. This group talked about marvelous spiritual experiences such as walking through rainbows. But when the leaders of that group tried to persuade us to begin selling various things to support the meetings, I never went back.

At the same time, I was attending a Young Life Bible study. It was easy to return to week after week (there were quite a few hot girls there). I made a lot of snide comments during the Bible studies—I think I was realizing that it wasn't the people but their faith I could not understand.

I stuck with Young Life—maybe because they never required anything of me and allowed me to doubt while encouraging me to ask more questions. And then one summer day about two months after graduation, it hit me. We were all sitting in Jack and Gretchen Boyd's living room just off Corey Road in Sylvania, Ohio. Several of us had just finished playing a game of basketball in the driveway. It was hot outside, and we were sweaty. The evening sun was low in the sky. Inside the house it was cooler. Twenty or so teenagers sat in chairs or on the floor, cross-legged or with knees hunched up like me. We were to listen to a tape of a talk on "love" by a guy named Bill Bright. I settled in, not very excited about it, and began daydreaming.

I thought of all the people who had ever loved me in the name of Jesus

in the short eighteen years of my life. They were like clouds in a clear blue
sky. Every cloud had the name of a Christ-follower on it. I could see water
start to pour out of each cloud, like a stream. Then all the streams flowing
out of each cloud converged into an airborne river, descending straight to-
ward the top of my head.

I watched with interest. And then something really weird happened. I
felt the water hit my head. Suddenly I was an empty jar being filled up. I
could feel the water rising inside my hollow legs, up past my hips, then up
toward my shoulders. It was a Spirit-meets-body experience.

When I was completely full to the top of my head, things changed
again. Now there was a geyser located somewhere in my chest, and the
water was shooting out of the top of my head. I was bursting with joy, and
I knew that Jesus was alive, that he was real. I knew that I was his.

I can't explain it to this day. One moment I didn't believe, the
next moment I did.

Things began to change after that. The Bible suddenly made
much more sense, as if it were a letter written to me. I enjoyed
reading it immensely. I had unanswered questions about evolu-
tion, the reliability of the Scriptures, the creation of the universe,
how a good God could allow suffering, that sort of thing. But I
was now looking at those questions from the other side. This was
the watershed of my life.

This preternatural conversion experience of mine is not the
norm. God deals with us each in ways that are best for us. John
Wesley, the founder of Methodism, experienced a "strange
warmth" in his heart as he discovered forgiveness in Christ. C. S.
Lewis was riding in the side-car of his brother's motorcycle; when
they left the house, he didn't believe in Jesus, but by the time they
arrived at the zoo, he did. (I wonder if it had to do with his
brother's driving, but I digress.) Some people feel a huge burden
lifted from their souls, some undergo a great joy, some simply see
things in a new light. I know people, raised in a Christian home,

who can't remember *not* believing. Don't judge your own conversion against anyone else's.

During college I got involved in Young Life leadership, eventually leading a club in my hometown after I had transferred from Miami University in Oxford, Ohio, to the University of Toledo. That meant that in addition to going to college and working a part-time job, I was spending time with high school kids on a weekly basis. I went to their football games and basketball games, took them out to lunch, and talked regularly with them on the phone about their lives. I told them about Jesus and asked how they were doing. And once a week, I would share a simple gospel message at a meeting in some student's home.

By the time I was twenty years old, I knew that I wanted to focus my energies on bringing the gospel to young people. I was so sure of this that I called the Young Life area director, Gary Burk, a beloved mentor of mine. We held our meeting at a Taco Bell in Toledo (home of the Mud Hens, Tony Paco's hot dogs and the glass capital of the world).

"Gary," I announced, "I know what I want to do for the rest of my life! I want to bring the message of Jesus Christ to young people! I want to be on Young Life staff!"

Gary, with his gray sideburns and in his profound wisdom, replied, "OK, Mike, but I don't want you to pursue ministry right out of college. I want you to go get a job. You need to work in a regular vocation so that you will understand what it's like for the people you're ministering to, and you'll better understand the people who are supporting you and what they have to go through."

I thought to myself, *I don't want to hear that! I've heard from God. I want to have fun working!* I sensed a call from God. But I had this impression that young adult ministry was all about hanging out with friends, playing disc golf with people, and going to restaurants and sporting events. Although my desires were set in stone,

I decided to follow godly counsel and authority and continued going to college. But I changed majors to become a teacher so I could still be around high school students.

Two years later at a YMCA pool where I worked as a lifeguard, I spotted a girl in the water and thought she was beautiful. (It was difficult to keep watching everyone else!) I eventually met her through another lifeguard who was dating her brother. Mary's parents had escaped from what was then Communist Czechoslovakia. They spoke Czech a lot at home. I was used to the immigrant experience from my own family, so we got along on that level. She was an artist and an English major, having just graduated from John Carroll University in Cleveland. She was on her way to get her master's degree at Purdue University. She was Catholic and had been part of a prayer group in high school. We found that we had our faith in common. We started dating and were married two years later at Gesu Catholic Church and the Holy Trinity Greek Orthodox Church in Toledo.

I had been teaching high school English for a couple years by then, but during our engagement I finally applied to be on Young Life staff. I went on staff in the lovely city of Cleveland, where several years before, the Cuyahoga River had caught on fire because it was so polluted. I should have taken that as a warning.

We didn't know how much I was going to get paid because Young Life in Cleveland had a financial problem. The paychecks had a little box in the bottom right-hand corner that read, "Salary in Arrears." In other words, "This is how much we owe you but can't pay you because the donations haven't come in yet." When the "Salary in Arrears" got to be substantial, Young Life closed down on the east side of Cleveland, and my wife and I had to leave.

We went back to Toledo and I taught again. At this point I was beginning to think, *God, you've given me this passion to spread the gospel to young people, and I can't do it!* I felt like a failure. Things weren't going very smoothly in our young marriage. I had taken a risk to follow Jesus and sank.

I licked my wounds and eventually got involved with a Charismatic church. Considering Mary's and my Greek Orthodox/Presbyterian/Catholic/Young Life history, I was thinking to myself, *What's a good evangelical boy like me doing in a charismatic church?* Still, the church believed strongly in the importance of discipleship, which we sorely needed.

The pastors said to me, "We believe that God has you here so we can speak into your life. You need to fix your marriage and other areas of life, because you're not quite ready for prime-time ministry." And so, again, I gave up my dreams of ministry and taught in a high school while working on a marriage that needed serious attention.

Then, joy of joys, our first daughter was born. Sixteen months later, her sister arrived. Soon after that it became clear that I was not making enough money in teaching, so I took up employment at a steel mill. I figured that since I wasn't doing ministry like I really wanted to, I might as well make a good hourly wage. In the four years I worked there I made a lot more money than I did teaching. I was obviously not in my ideal occupation, however. I just could not concentrate on the tasks at hand. I was bored out of my mind. I almost got killed a few times. One day, my supervisor came up to me and said something like, "Sares, you're a klutz! You're a danger, not just to yourself, but also to the whole crew. Keep your mind on your work!"

One night I took a bunch of kids from my church to a concert. I sat in the back of the venue while the kids scattered around the concert hall. I listened to song after song all by myself, with nothing in particular going on in my mind, when suddenly, out of nowhere, I heard a voice—loud, but not audible: "Mike, someday, a band like that will come out of your ministry."

I knew there was no one near me, but I turned around just to make sure. There was no one there for rows and rows. I thought, *God? Are you talking to me? Are you trying to say something to me?* I had a strong feeling I had just heard from the Lord, but that kind of thing just doesn't happen very often!

God doesn't give supernatural words capriciously. I have come to believe that I received a divine word from him because I was going to need it. There was still much he had to accomplish in my life and character before I was ready for the ministry trials ahead. It came down to living what I had long prayed, "I want to know Christ and the power of his resurrection and the fellowship of sharing in his sufferings" (Phil 3:10).

I naturally began looking around me for evidence of this promise. The kids in the youth group started a garage band that never got out of the garage—and I was disappointed.

After four years of boredom, I realized that I had no idea why I was still at the steel mill, so I quit. I was willing to do anything else. I went on to be a salesman with a specialty printing company run by Christians. Eventually I got into advertising and got laid off. I worked in radio sales and wrote commercials for the station, washed package cars for UPS and then returned to being a salesman with the same printing company as before—all the while doing ministry on the side, all the while wondering about the voice I had heard.

I began a college ministry at the University of Toledo after work. I kept asking God where his promise about some band was going to appear. "Is it these students? These guys? God, where is it?"

Several years passed. I was slowly losing steam for anything except ministry. I was crying out to God: "Where is it? Let me at the dream! I'm full of passion!" And there was nothing. Meanwhile, I felt as if a part of me was dying in a job that became more and more difficult to accomplish. I had gone from being in the top 10 percent of sticker salesmen nationwide to below average. I went from shop to shop and tried to get excited about the fact that I was selling pieces of paper with glue on them.

By this time I had four kids and a mortgage, and I hated my life. I would actually weep with the frustration of it. I remember crying on Mary's shoulder as I left for work, barely able to muster the energy to go and sell yet another day. I was a pathetic mess. During that time, I had my "quiet times"—devotional times with God in silence and solitude—in the car on my one-hour commute to work and back. On the way to my sales territory I would be crying, "You've got to do something, God. I'm just dying here. This is horrible. I have all this passion and vision for ministry, for your people, and it's like I'm doing nothing. I don't want to do this sales job anymore. It's just about the money and it's not enough!"

On my way back I would spend my "quiet time" screaming at God. "What is wrong with you? Are you some kind of a mean God that enjoys watching me squirm? Either change my heart or change my circumstances! One or the other! Because I have this passion and I am suffering."

I blamed God for everything. He was the one making me suffer. I didn't realize then what I know now: unless a seed falls to the ground and dies, it cannot produce any fruit (Jn 12:24).

What do you do when God has you in the middle of a desert with no water? All there is to do is hold on like Job. "Though he slay me," Job declared, "yet will I hope in him" (Job 13:15). You join the patriarch Joseph, languishing in a prison cell in Egypt, hoping against hope that dreams would one day come true. You join Jesus. The writer of the book of Hebrews says that Jesus "learned obedience from what he suffered" (Heb 5:8). Could it be that vision, passion and suffering are closely related?

I remember when I was at my breaking point in the sales job.

My sales figures were tumbling quickly. I had no passion for selling at all. My sales manager was a Christian. His assistant was
there in the office with him when I said, "Guys, all those dreams
I had for ministry, I am nailing them in a coffin and I'm burying
them six feet under. I am going to be a salesman first, foremost
and always."

I got up and turned to walk out of the room and they said,
"Stop! Sit down." They both came over to the chair where I had
seated myself. I had no idea what they were going to do. Would
they fire me right then and there? Would they put me on some
kind of probation?

Instead, they stood on either side of me, placed their hands on
my shoulders and prayed for me. "God, blow down doors of opportunity for Mike to get where you've created him to be."

I could hardly believe my ears. A subsequent meeting with the
president of the company confirmed their intentions to assist me
in getting to where I had long believed I should be: in ministry.

At this stage of my life, I was thirty-nine years old. By the time
I was forty, my wife and kids and I were in our car heading toward Colorado so that I could attend Denver Seminary.

3

Spectacle

What Churches Should Look Like

*We have been made a spectacle to the whole
universe, to angels as well as to men.*

Once we arrived in Colorado and I was enrolled in seminary, I began looking for a part-time job in a church. I landed a position as a singles ministry director in a traditional Presbyterian church in the Capitol Hill District called Corona.

Shortly after I arrived, I met Dennis. He was a little too young to fit in with most of the single adults that were there, but we developed a bond very quickly. He was a graduate of the University of Denver with a degree in business and hotel management. He was working as head of customer service for the night shift at the Westin Hotel downtown. In essence, he was a yuppie, but he was also a great musician. He played both the guitar and bass well, had a good voice, noodled on the piano, and had played trombone all through high school and college.

Dennis loved eating breakfast at local greasy-spoon diners, and he introduced me to a few of them. During our breakfasts we would discuss his life and matters of theology. At one meeting, we were talking about how one hears from God. I responded with all of the standard pastoral examples.

"Well Dennis, the first place we hear God speak is through the Scripture, but he can also speak to us through trusted mentors and friends. Scripture tells us God speaks to us through the wonder of nature."

Dennis looked at me and asked quite sincerely, "Yeah, but does God ever talk to people today the way he used to in the Bible? I mean audibly or almost audibly."

I felt a little paralyzed. I wanted to say yes but then I knew where the conversation might lead. I thought about it for a moment and then said very slowly, "Yes, I believe that he does speak that way."

"Well, has God ever spoken to you that way?" he asked.

"Yes," I told him.

"What did he say to you?"

I related the story about the voice telling me that someday a band would come out of my ministry. Dennis was wide-eyed, incredulous. Then he said with great enthusiasm, "I'm sticking around you, then!"

During the first year of my tenure it became painfully obvious that in order to have an effective singles ministry, we would have to divide the group by age. This is not unusual, so we had a forty-something group and a thirty-something group. But then an odd thing happened: younger singles started coming to church.

It began innocently enough with a few twenty-year-olds checking out a neighborhood church. I introduced myself one Sunday and found out that they were involved with a fledgling ska band. I didn't know what that was at the time, but imagine

Jamaican rhythms at punk speed with a horn section. I asked when their next concert was and told them I'd try to stop by. They were thinking, *Yeah, right. He won't show.* But I did.

I went to a second concert, taking Dennis along. I remember standing in the back with Dennis, watching the band perform. There was a lot of energy in the room. Kids were dancing, and it seemed like the whole floor was bouncing in rhythm. I playfully elbowed Dennis and shouted into his ear, "They don't have a trombone player." He responded, "Trombone gigs are hard to come by!"

After the concert, I chatted with some of the band members and then with the concert promoter. When it was time to leave, I couldn't find Dennis. I looked everywhere. Finally, he emerged from a back room. On the way back to the car, he informed me that he had secured an audition with the band. The following week Dennis was welcomed into the group, becoming its missing piece. The band was now complete with vocals, drums, bass, two guitars, a trumpet, sax and Dennis.

Five Iron Frenzy's popularity soon soared. As time went by I found myself blurring the line between pastor and default band manager. Multiple Christian record labels expressed interest. At the time they seemed to have either lots of money and little integrity or plenty of integrity and no money. My goal was to make sure they signed with a record label that put ministry before profit, yet ran a sound business as well. Our prayers were answered in Frank Tate and 5 Minute Walk Records.

With that goal accomplished, I turned my attention to more pastoral duties. I continued to develop relationships with band members and their friends. They began a Bible study to which they would invite people who attended their concerts. As the band's fan base grew, it became apparent that the Bible study needed to move out of an apartment and into a church building.

I volunteered the basement of the church, and suddenly I was responsible for a burgeoning twenty-something ministry. I became the host pastor while Reese Roper, Five Iron Frenzy's lyricist and lead singer, led the study.

As time went by, people from the Bible study became interested in attending our Presbyterian church service. They had two choices: a contemporary service at 8:30 a.m. (aimed at people their parents' age) or a traditional service at 11 a.m. with full liturgy, geared toward their grandparents. The extra two-and-a-half hours of sleep was sufficient motivation to bring most of them to the later service. So come Sunday morning, a number of young adults with tattoos, various body piercings and neon-dyed hair found their seats in the back of the church, while senior citizens with costume jewelry and lavender rinses in their gray hair sat up in the front, in their time-honored seats.

It was beautiful. *This is what churches should look like,* I thought.

The number of young adults remained relatively small. I realized that those who were coming on Sunday morning were making a huge cultural leap into a foreign environment. Meanwhile, the Bible study was becoming ingrown. The interaction was good, but it just wasn't for everyone. Discussions were intense, passionate and long. Sometimes the conversation got so heated, you'd think they were angry with each other! So I suggested we start an alternate service for twenty-somethings.

Roper's initial reaction to my idea was "Sounds great, Mike." Then I told him that I wanted him to start it with me. This request was met with a substantial "No." But I got him to promise that he would pray about it.

After a few months I finally got an affirmative answer from Reese, but his touring schedule prevented us from actually beginning for over a year. We did, however, have a trial run. We invited everyone who had ever come to the Bible study and made a general announcement to the young adults at church. About twenty-five people showed up. I was amazed. I couldn't believe what God was doing right before our eyes. This was just a trial run, and our plan was to begin in earnest after the holidays. But things for me were about to change drastically.

The church where I had been on staff for five years had hired a new senior pastor a year before. In October, the new pastor asked me to resign my position with Corona.

The congregation put on a generous gala farewell party for me and my family. It was a bittersweet experience. It's a wonderful thing to listen as people express their gratitude for the work you have waited all your adult life to do, but I had no idea where I was going to find work to support my family. I was not finished with seminary, and my mortgage payment loomed large.

During one of my last days at the church, a woman from the congregation came into my office and told me something I had a difficult time accepting. She was aware of my forced resignation and told me that I would come to see this event as God's kiss on my forehead. I thought she was crazy. I had been kissed on the forehead continually as I grew up. Greeks tend to kiss a lot. It was always a sign of great affection from my grandparents, my parents, my uncles and my aunts. Being fired felt *nothing* like that.

My immediate goal became to find the highest paying pastorate within the will of God. I was offered positions as a singles pastor in Pennsylvania and Virginia, but neither my family nor I felt right about moving. My efforts to find a position in Denver were fruitless.

In November, I went on a prayer retreat with a good friend, Steve Garcia. He asked, "If someone gave you the money to do anything, what would you do?" I knew immediately. I would continue the vision of creating a church service for those who did

not fit in—a church for the left-out. But money remained a huge
issue. I wrote the following in a prayer journal that day:

> OK . . . this is the deal, Lord. You're the boss. I am the em-
> ployee. I'll do my best for what you want done, but you're
> responsible to pay me. I'm not going to worry about the
> money. I simply cannot if I'm to do my job. Can't do both.
> The reason I was effective before is because I got paid regu-
> larly. I would love to try and be effective again, but I need
> to know that you'll take care of my family so that I can go
> about your business. I don't know how you're going to do it,
> but I'll be watching.

I sketched out a rough idea of what this church might look like
and showed it to Steve. He got excited and shared the vision with
the leadership team at his church. In the meantime, my brother
and a close friend came to me, independently of one another, and
told me that they would help support me financially if I would
continue pursuing the vision God had given me for reaching the
left-out. Steve returned from his church leadership meeting offering support of a thousand dollars a month for a year. All of a sudden I had a part-time salary with no employer and a job that existed only in my head.

Reese, Mary and I invited everybody from the Bible study to
a brainstorming session. About a dozen people showed up. We
now think of it as the birthday of Scum of the Earth
Church—02.02.2000.

The meeting was sandwiched between dinner together and
watching one of my favorite movies, *Groundhog Day*, starring Bill
Murray, about a guy who keeps getting second chances to be the
man he has no idea that he really wants to be. At the beginning of
the meeting, I asked a simple but important question: If you were
to create a church that would be the kind of place in which you

could be yourself, to which you could invite friends and they'd feel comfortable, what would it look like?

Sunday night worship with a basic message

Wednesday night in-depth Bible Study

No cliques

A welcoming, loving environment with no one left out because of looks or actions or sin

A ministry and leadership team that goes out and invites people along with members of the church

Homeless people; anybody is welcome

We have to "target" somebody, though we can't be too broad

The place of worship can't have stuff like silk flowers, pictures of Jesus, religious banners and podiums

The arts should be highly visible—a strong focus on music, dance, literature, poetry, visual art, etc.

Worship should also be a time of fellowship with coffee, doughnuts, etc.

No Christianese. Stay away from words like fellowship. Use "hang-out-time" instead.

Have a meal after the service

Worship service can't start too early

Anyone may serve in some kind of ministry

No offering basket passed. No pressure to give money

Monthly expenditures are published

Church gives money away to those in need

50/50 giving practiced (just donate half of what you give to the church
   —other half given to a charity or ministry of your choice)

Individuals are encouraged to give money to each other as each has a
   need

Not the same preacher every week

Women and men teach

Open up worship team each week to additional musicians and singers
   besides the core group

Before the church service, walk around neighborhood and invite people to
   an open forum at the end to argue and ask questions

Be real and transparent

Follow up on people who decide to follow Jesus with discipleship training
   (perhaps same gender follows up)

Throw a party for people who decide to follow Jesus

Have communion

Don't use the words Genx. or alternative in relation to the church

Music shouldn't be trendy or forced but down-to-earth

A variety of musical style should be employed

Spirit-led music is a must

Liffey (Sares' dog) should be the church mascot

Have enough small groups and Bible studies for all who want them

Sometimes organize separate men's and women's meetings

No singles groups

Tolerance: diversity in nonessentials, unity in essentials of the faith

Facility should have lots of space for dance

Don't build on a foundation of rebellion, but on God

Be respectful of other churches

Do things with other churches

Bulletin should be like a 'zine

A 'zine as an outreach tool

Church should be computer friendly with a website and e-mail

Use everyone's talents

Church should not be big on authority but love

The congregation's authority would balance out any hierarchy

The church would pray

A reverse pyramid of authority: leadership should not be at the top but at the bottom, serving the congregation and equipping the saints for their own ministries

Don't spread ourselves too thin; develop a main focus

Need committed people

Spay or neuter animals that wander into the building

Mashed potato eating contest!

No more apples in the vending machine, please

Brad gives everyone a piggyback ride

Welcoming posse @ church, perhaps handing out loaves of bread

Whatever building we end up in is open all the time

Teams of people after the services to meet with those in need

Pastors are pastored and held accountable

We need to dialogue about whether we'll have pastors and staff at some point

A church that speaks to both married and single issues

Tailor the services to whomever the Lord brings

*A preaching team meets with the speakers to discuss effectiveness of
messages*

High school and middle school ministries to come later

Obviously, we had a lot of fun at the meeting. Some of the
responses surprised me. Others were funny. A few were even profound. A lot of the ideas made it into the fabric of the church,
while some of them did not. But everyone left feeling ownership
of what God was doing in our midst.

We had several such meetings before actually opening up services in late March. At one of those meetings, the issue finally
came up of what to name our "church for left-out." I had some
names in mind ever since my retreat, where I had been calling
this ministry Chi-Ro Nights (from the first two Greek letters of
the word for Christ, Cristos.) Other names emerged from the
people gathered there in my living room: The Cave, The Dregs,
Haven, The Iconoclasts, J2K, B.O.B (Bunch of Believers).

Then Reese spoke up. He had thought for a few years that
Scum of the Earth would be a great name for a group such as this.
And he was sure it was in the Bible . . . somewhere . . . he didn't
know just where.

Standing up front by the flip-chart, marker in my hand, having just written down all the other ideas for a name, I watched
this latest entry flicker in the minds of the group. Then I could
see it burn even more brightly in their eyes. A few didn't like it,
but most did.

As the official moderator of the meeting I tried everything in
my power to sway the group in another direction. I told Reese
that he would have to find the phrase in the Bible—even though

I had a pretty good idea about where it was! It comes from 1 Cor-inthians, where Paul is describing the life of faith that he and the other apostles were living:

> For it seems to me that God has put us apostles on display at the end of the procession, like men condemned to die in the arena. We have been made a spectacle to the whole universe, to angels as well as to men. We are fools for Christ, but you are so wise in Christ! We are weak, but you are strong! You are honored, we are dishonored! To this very hour we go hungry and thirsty, we are in rags, we are brutally treated, we are homeless. We work hard with our own hands. When we are cursed, we bless; when we are persecuted, we endure it; when we are slandered, we answer kindly. Up to this mo-ment we have become the scum of the earth, the refuse of the world. (1 Cor 4:9-13)

Still, I was not in favor of the name. Perhaps I was afraid of it. Maybe I was too insecure to lead a church with a name like that. What would my family and friends think? So I used an old Chris-tian tactic to buy myself some time: I had everyone pray about it for a week before making the final decision. (Yes, I can be that big of a poser, I am ashamed to admit.) In the meantime, I called my mentor and friend Rich Hurst, whose book *Getting Real* was the blueprint for starting this ministry.

"Rich, they want to name the church Scum of the Earth!"

"Mike," he replied, "don't let them do it!"

The next week we met, and it was a done deal. "Scum of the Earth" became the name for our attempt at doing church. It was the best decision I never made.

4

𝕽isk

Faith, Failure & Following Jesus

We are fools for Christ, but you are so wise in Christ!

*W*hen I was very young my mother would drive me to swimming lessons. She and the other parents would watch through a glass window while our instructor taught us the basics of water safety. During one of our first lessons, at the deep end of the pool, the swim teacher asked which of us wanted to be a "guinea pig." I raised my hand. I would demonstrate buoyancy to the rest of the class by jumping into the deep water. I jumped in and eventually made it back to the surface, where the instructor had a long pole for me to grab onto.

After the lesson was over and I was in the car going home, my mother turned to me, a bit flustered, and asked, "Do you even know what a guinea pig is?" The truth was that I did not. "Then why did you volunteer?" she inquired. She must have been afraid that I wouldn't come up from under the water. I think I just wanted to see what would happen if I raised my hand.

In the Bible, there is a much more dramatic story involving water, risk and failure. Jesus has told the disciples to go on ahead of him across the lake in a boat while he stays back on shore to pray a little longer. As they begin making their way across the lake, a storm suddenly descends on them. The Gospel of Matthew tells what happens next:

> During the fourth watch of the night Jesus went out to them, walking on the lake. When the disciples saw him walking on the lake, they were terrified. "It's a ghost," they said, and cried out in fear.
>
> But Jesus immediately said to them: "Take courage! It is I. Don't be afraid."
>
> "Lord, if it's you," Peter replied, "tell me to come to you on the water."
>
> "Come," he said.
>
> Then Peter got down out of the boat, walked on the water and came toward Jesus. But when he saw the wind, he was afraid and, beginning to sink, cried out, "Lord, save me!"
>
> Immediately Jesus reached out his hand and caught him. "You of little faith," he said, "why did you doubt?"
>
> And when they climbed into the boat, the wind died down. Then those who were in the boat worshiped him, saying, "Truly you are the Son of God." (Mt 14:25-33)

Most of the times that I hear this story in church, the preacher is talking about faith—specifically, Peter's lack of it when he sinks, and our lack of it in our day-to-day lives. If only we have more faith, we are implored, then we can do amazing things like Jesus. Fine; that's true. But I relate more to Peter than to Jesus in this story, and he appears to have sunk.

"Lord, if it's you, tell me to come to you" is what Peter said.

Just what is going through Peter's mind, I wonder? Is he thinking, *It would be really cool to walk on the water!* Maybe. Perhaps he is thinking something else though, something like, *We're in a terrible storm. This is bad. The ship is going to sink. It's safest to be with Jesus.*

He steps onto the surface of the lake, and it supports him! Then he gets afraid. I picture this like a dream sequence in a movie.

There is no moon, there are no stars. The roar of the wind and the waves is deafening. Peter's feet won't move. It is a fisherman's worst nightmare as he starts to sink. He cries out to Jesus to save him. Jesus does.

If I were Peter I would have been shaking. I would have been relieved. Eventually, I am sure, I would be so grateful just for the experience of having walked on water with Jesus even for a little while. At that particular moment though, wet and cold and having just had a brush with death, I'd be looking for words of assurance from my Lord and Savior.

Peter hears a mild rebuke instead: "You of little faith, why did you doubt?" It is a tiny correction by the teacher, but I'd be ticked off, embarrassed in front of the rest of the disciples and my former fishing buddies.

I relate more to Peter than anyone else in this story. Moving to Colorado at forty years old with my wife and four children was no picnic. We sold our house for about the same amount of money for which it was purchased. We cashed out the little retirement we had saved, rented a truck and packed everything in it. For Mary, it was especially hard. She had worked things out with Jesus well before we arrived in Denver, and although it had been a process, she knew that we were both called to move to Colorado. She wasn't pursuing her vocation by moving to Denver, however; she was leaving it.

All through our marriage, Mary had been teaching literature and humanities part-time at the college level. She never found that same work again. She left her house to go live with my brother and his wife. She left her family and friendships that were fifteen years deep. We arrived in Denver with no jobs, no health insurance and no clue as to what Jesus was going to do.

But we had faith that we were following Christ, and we had the support of both of my brothers and their wives who lived in Colorado. We also found kindness among the people at Denver Seminary. Dr. James Means, a senior professor there, talked honestly about the hardships that pastors face and illustrated them with stories from his own life and ministry. Dr. Means was my mentor during the time I was being let go from Corona Presbyterian and then during the time I was deciding what to do next. We used to meet at a bagel shop and discuss what was going on in my life.

At one point, I had a couple of offers from large churches to come and be a pastor for their single adults. I told Dr. Means about those possibilities, and then I shared my belief that God was up to something with the skaters and punks with whom I'd been working in the Capitol Hill District of Denver.

Dr. Means thought for a while and then opened up about his own life. He had been called to a small church in the suburbs of Denver some forty years before; had he not accepted the position it would have undoubtedly gone to someone else. The church would have chosen another pastor who preached the gospel, he said, and because of the church's location and the growth of the population of Denver at that time, the church would have surely grown even as it had under his guidance. And then he said, "Maybe it would have done better with someone else than with me."

Twenty years ago, he went on to say, the seminary asked him to become its professor of pastoral ministries. He accepted the position; but if he hadn't, the seminary would have chosen some-one else. And then quite humbly he added, "Perhaps they would have chosen someone better qualified than me."

Then he shifted in his chair and lowered his voice. "But you know, Mike, when I go to Africa and teach pastoral students in a grass-roofed hut or when I'm with the medical missions team there and am inoculating African babies against disease, I know when I'm on the plane returning to the United States that no one is going back to take my place."

Then he stopped talking and looked at me.

I don't know if you've ever experienced those long pauses where the first one to speak loses, but I understood exactly what he was saying. If I didn't accept the megachurch positions that I was being offered, then undoubtedly someone else would come along and fill those roles. But if I didn't go and minister to those who were the "left-out" in the Capitol Hill District, then no one else was going to take my place. Sitting in the bagel shop, Dr. Means was gently challenging me to risk everything again for the sake of following Christ.

I sensed Jesus saying, "Come to me on the waters," but all I was thinking was, *You're painting me into a corner!* How could I possibly do this to my family? I needed the security of a large organization and a steady paycheck. Our daughters were getting ready to enter college. Our sons were eating so much food that I had to start recognizing them by the pants they wore, since the top half of each son was almost always in the refrigerator. My wife had already given up so much to move to Colorado.

I left that meeting in turmoil. I now sensed Jesus asking me to take a risk, the effect of which might be devastating. I needed time to think and pray and wrestle through several questions.

The first question of discernment is always whether what we feel compelled to do is within the parameters of Scripture. When I worked in the steel mill, I met a guy who liked to seduce other men's wives. It was exciting for him because he knew he was taking a huge risk. That risk, however, lies outside the boundary of one of God's commandments: "You shall not commit adultery" (Ex 20:14).

When it came to the risk I was facing, however, the answer was just as obvious. Mission work, church planting, spreading the good news about Jesus to those who have never heard it—these things are well within the limits of Scripture, and as a matter of fact, Jesus seems to like that kind of thing!

> Jesus came and told his disciples, "I have been given all authority in heaven and on earth. Therefore, go and make disciples of all the nations, baptizing them in the name of the Father and the Son and the Holy Spirit. Teach these new disciples to obey all the commands I have given you. And be sure of this: I am with you always, even to the end of the age." (Mt 28:18-20 NLT)

So, I knew my question was within the parameter of Scripture. But there was a second question I had to face. Were significant people in my life encouraging me to take this particular risk? Dr. Means made his position clear, but what about the others?

Mary knew that our family shouldn't move again so quickly, so any ministry I worked with had to keep us in Denver. Beyond that, she simply trusted me to figure it out. I had been pledged support for this effort independently from a variety of sources: my best friend, Paul; my two brothers, Matt and Mark; and my friend Steve Garcia, speaking on behalf of his church. I was being encouraged by those whose opinions I respected to take the risk of continuing to work with the people who would eventually make up Scum of the Earth.

The third question I had to ask myself before taking a big risk was about my own heart. Plumbing the depths of one's own heart is scary business. The Old Testament prophet Jeremiah observed,

The heart is deceitful above all things
   and beyond cure.
Who can understand it? (Jer 17:9)

Sometimes I know the right thing to do, but I'm in turmoil
because I don't want to do it. Other times, guilt is the only moti-
vating factor. Then there are times that my willingness to take
risks is being compelled by spiritual pride or even selfishness.
These heart issues had to be sifted through the fabric of my conscience. This takes time alone with God, and that time alone for
me came in the process of a personal retreat.

Only the Lord can reveal to us the truth about our motivations.
King David prayed to God about this, saying,

Test me, O LORD, and try me,
   examine my heart and my mind;
for your love is ever before me. (Ps 26:2-3)

The book of Proverbs gives us a metaphor about the testing and
refining of our heart's motives:

The crucible for silver and the furnace for gold,
   but the LORD tests the heart. (Prov 17:3)

During that time with the Lord, I fasted for the greater portion
of the day, read Scripture and took long walks speaking to God
out loud. I'd ask him the questions that were on my heart. I didn't
expect God to speak audibly; I just wanted a peace that put my
fears at rest.

That retreat was a turning point. I knew that what I was about
to risk was within the parameters of Scripture. I knew that my
trusted counselors were encouraging me to take it. And I came
back from my retreat believing that, with the Lord's help, I was
up to the task.

Specifically, I was up for the possibility of failure. That was why I had been struggling so hard with the decision. None of us wants to fail. I sure didn't, as my failure would affect my family and those I was attempting to lead. I was afraid of failing; but during the retreat, I decided that I was more afraid of not attempting to follow Jesus.

Any risk-taking adventure includes the possibility of failure— of falling flat on your face, of looking like an idiot to your friends, to the angels and to the Lord. And you've got to be okay with that. This is the paradoxical thing: you're going to sink, at least up to your neck, just so Jesus can say to you, "You of little faith. Why did you doubt?"

Several years and many swimming lessons after my experience as a guinea pig (not to mention a swimming merit badge in Boy Scouts), my family was on vacation at a lake in Michigan. My father, my brother Mark and I were in a rowboat in the middle of the lake. I decided that even though the lake was very large and the water very deep, I could swim to the other shore. Without warning, I stood up in the boat, announced my intentions and dove off.

My father was incredulous; my brother was shocked. When I surfaced (hooray for buoyancy), my dad had a twinkle in his eye. "So, you're going to swim to the other side, huh? OK then, Mark and I will meet you over on shore. See you soon!" And with that, he began to slowly row away.

Things were great for a short time. I was exhilarated and up to the challenge. Soon, though, my skinny arms and legs began to grow tired. The rowboat was pulling away, and I got worried. I called out to my father, "Dad! Come back! I don't want to swim to the other side anymore."

"You don't want to give up so soon, do you?" he answered.

I treaded water in the cold lake. "Please! I don't think I could make it!" With that, he turned the boat around and picked me up.

Failure is always an option. If it were not, there would be no such thing as taking a risk. But our idea of failure and our Father's are different sometimes. Peter risked walking on water and failed at it quickly, to be sure. But Jesus was there to catch him. We can fail in our own eyes, but his purposes in us and in the world are accomplished nonetheless.

So often I have imagined the Lord saying those same words to me, as I have risked and failed many times. It's not all success, power and prestige in this life. It just isn't. The point we often miss is that Peter was actually safer on the lake in a storm with Jesus than in the boat with the rest of his friends. He heard those corrective words from Jesus, to be sure; but Peter learned something that none of the others learned that day because he took a risk.

The apostle Paul was also a risk-taker for Jesus. He put his life on the line for the cause of Christ.

> Whatever was to my profit I now consider loss for the sake of Christ. What is more, I consider everything a loss compared to the surpassing greatness of knowing Christ Jesus my Lord, for whose sake I have lost all things. I consider them rubbish. . . .
>
> I want to know Christ and the power of his resurrection and the fellowship of sharing in his sufferings, becoming like him in his death, and so, somehow, to attain to the resurrection from the dead. Not that I have already obtained all this, or have already been made perfect, but I press on to take hold of that for which Christ Jesus took hold of me. (Phil 3:7-8, 10-12)

Perhaps no other of the early apostles traveled as far and endured as much as Paul in spreading the good news about Jesus. At the end of his life he was jailed for his efforts and faced execution under the Roman Emperor Nero. Church tradition tells us that this apostle to the Gentiles was led forth from his prison cell just outside of Rome and beheaded.

I wonder how he felt as he was being led to have his head cut off. His letters from prison lead me to believe he was a hardy sort of man. Did he begin to sink as the moment of his execution arrived? Maybe. But immediately upon sinking into the waters of his own death, he rose to find himself present with the Lord.

What about the apostle Peter? Peter made a habit of risk. He was the first one to say that Jesus was the Messiah, that he was the Christ. Peter grabbed a crippled man's hand and miraculously healed him. Those were risks. He could have looked like a false prophet at either point, but he took the risk he heard Jesus asking him to take.

There was something about Peter's risk-taking personality that made Jesus say of him, "On this rock I will build my church" (Mt 16:18). Jesus can build on people who take risks, who believe enough to try something for his kingdom.

I wonder what happened on the shore after it was all over, after Peter walked on water, then stumbled, then was helped by Jesus. I picture the disciples cooking fish, Peter drying off. Jesus looks over at Peter and smiles and winks. Peter looks up and nods his head. That's a wink and a smile that nobody else could share except Peter and Jesus.

When we take these risks for the kingdom, we get relationship. We get a depth of relationship with God that we didn't have before. Could it be that one of the avenues to deeper relationship with Jesus is taking the risks that Jesus asks you to take—following him where he bids you to follow?

God never fails. For those of us who take the risk of following him, that is a great comfort. Even if beginning Scum of the Earth Church had ended up in complete abject failure and humiliation for me, Jesus would have used that to increase my faith in him and my relationship with him—and then asked me to risk it all over again. Our relationship all the stronger and more vibrant, we would have walked into the next adventure. As the Scriptures promise, every risk God calls us to is one that he accompanies us through.

5

Shift

Paying Attention to the Voice of God

Therefore judge nothing before the appointed time;
wait till the Lord comes.

*E*arly on at Scum of the Earth, we held the evening meal smack dab in the middle of the service. (Eventually we moved the meal to before church, but after several years we moved it back to the middle of the service.) The young founding members wanted the meal to be sacred, a time of sharing our lives over supper. Some of them had experienced the store-bought-cookies-and-mediocre-coffee "fellowship time" after church while they grew up. They wanted something more intimate. We would sing worship songs for about half an hour, take a break to eat, and then go back to sing a few more songs and listen to the message.

One night during supper, a fight broke out between two young men, a goth and a punk, about something that had happened earlier that week on the streets of Capitol Hill. Punches were being thrown and clothes being torn when someone came and found me. By the time I arrived downstairs, a visiting pastor had broken up the fight, but the two assailants were fleeing the building.

I could see who they were, and I knew them both. This wasn't a brawl between strangers. They had become acquainted through Scum of the Earth, and both were following Jesus to the best of their abilities (which at the moment left a lot to be desired). I ran outside, caught up with one and asked him to wait for me to return. I found the other one hiding behind a dumpster down the street. I called him out (which took a little time) and then walked back with him while he told me his side of the story.

I was no stranger to fighting. After breaking up a scuffle between me and my brother, my father would require us to say, "I'm sorry," and kiss each other on the cheek. It was only after completing the reconciliation process with my brother that I could then hug and kiss dad.

I had dealt with this kind of thing before with my own four children too. Whether I had entered the girls' bedroom to find them screaming and pulling out each other's hair, or whether I was forced to step between my two sons before things got ugly, the Lord had prepared me for such a time as this fight between a goth and a punk.

Nevertheless, my professors at seminary hadn't prepared me for the possibility of a fight breaking out in the middle of church. At times like these, I often pray in the back of my mind, "Jesus, what are you up to here? I know that you've allowed this to happen in front of me for a purpose. How should I respond? What do you want us to learn?"

After a prayer like that, I mentally scan through the template of Scripture to see if God has said anything about situations like this before, trusting the Holy Spirit to answer my prayer by bringing the passage to my mind. This presumes, of course, that I've read the passage beforehand. I'm sure the Holy Spirit could just pop a verse into my head that I've never read before, but there are plenty of times the writers of the Bible—under the inspiration of the Spirit—adjure us to read, study and meditate upon Scripture in the first place.

In the case of what has now become known as "Fight Night" at Scum of the Earth, the passage that came to me was from the Gospel of Matthew. Jesus is talking about conflict resolution in a few different kinds of relationships:

> You're familiar with the command to the ancients, "Do not murder." I'm telling you that anyone who is so much as angry with a brother or sister is guilty of murder. Carelessly call a brother "idiot!" and you just might find yourself hauled into court. Thoughtlessly yell "stupid!" at a sister and you are on the brink of hellfire. The simple moral fact is that words kill. This is how I want you to conduct yourself in these matters. If you enter your place of worship and, about to make an offering, you suddenly remember a grudge a friend has against you, abandon your offering, leave immediately, go to this friend and make things right. Then and only then, come back and work things out with God. (Mt 5:21-24 *The Message*)

There is an important shift going on here. Jesus is taking his followers to a new level. They thought they were okay by following God's commandment not to murder others, even if they felt that they had reason to do so. Jesus refocuses their attention not on their actions but on their attitudes. He is saying, in effect, that they are doing well not to murder, but they would be doing better by not speaking murderously. It's a good thing to worship God by bringing an offering; it was back then, and it still is now. But it was, and is, a better thing to make things right with your friend first. Jesus had shifted peoples' priorities back in the first century, and he was doing the same thing twenty centuries later on Fight Night.

On the sidewalk outside the meeting place, I led these two in reconciliation. Each of them had to confess his own shortcomings and forgive the other's before I would let them go back inside. If I remember correctly, the goth guy ended up kneeling down on the concrete and kissing the punk's boots while declaring his repentance. Watching him prostrate himself before the guy with whom he had just started a fight was more than I had expected. I just shrugged my shoulders and said something profound like, "Well, uh . . . okay . . . if you really feel like you need to do that . . ."

Shifts are a hallmark of church history. At age nineteen Isaac Watts felt as if he were plodding through the metric hymns of the English church. He asked, "Where can you find a psalm that speaks of the miracles of wisdom and power as they are discovered in a crucified Christ?" His father, perhaps with a twinkle in his eye, encouraged him to see what he could do to "mend the matter." The result was the hymn *Behold the Glories of the Lamb,* the first of almost seven hundred hymns that Watts would pen during his lifetime, including the lyrics to *Joy to the World* and *When I Survey the Wondrous Cross.*

Not every English church immediately warmed up to young Isaac's newfangled hymns, however. Churches split over whether or not to sing "Watts's flights of fancy." Pastors were fired. Sometimes shifting to follow where Jesus is leading causes unpleasant side effects.

With the launch of Scum of the Earth, I began my own shift. The first time we opened worship services to the friends of those who had dreamed up the church, we were gathered in the converted living room of an old house in Capitol Hill, next to notorious Colfax Avenue. The place had been turned into a drop-in coffeehouse for street kids, but it still looked more like somebody's home than a Starbucks. There were around twenty people in attendance. Most sat on the hard wooden floor, a few sat on the couch or on the kitchen counter. Deva and Chris, two of the people who had helped dream up this new ministry, were sitting cross-legged on the floor, playing guitars cradled in their laps and leading us in singing. There was an overhead projector shining its distended rectangle of light on an old screen that had been re-paired with some wire. I felt like I was back in the 1970s, getting ready to speak at a Young Life Club.

Reese and I met the next week to debrief. "What happened to you?" he asked.

"What are you talking about?"

"Your sermon didn't sound like you at all. It sounded like you were trying to impress someone at my mom's church." I was clueless.

"Why don't you just talk to us like you talk to me over coffee? You need to sound like yourself. We like Mike. I don't know who you were trying to be."

I felt like I had been frozen stiff and was beginning to thaw. By the time Scum began I was already forty-six years old. There was no way I was going to try to look and speak like I was in my twenties. Trying too hard to be cool is the most uncool thing you can do. I didn't have any tattoos before Scum started, and I still don't. I've been told that my wearing cargo shorts is a young-adult fashion faux pas, even in the summer. And I've only dyed my hair neon blue a couple times, just for fun (using temporary dye, by the way). But Reese wasn't asking me to change the way I looked. It seemed like he was calling me back to something I'd known from before I got involved in the Christian subculture. He was asking me to be myself.

The great thing about new church plants is that when they are first formed, Christians there often still talk and dress the same way as the rest of their friends outside the church culture. (That is also one of the not-so-great things about church plants.) There are things we need to shift about ourselves when following Jesus; but there are also things we shouldn't. There is no shifting from the Ten Commandments. There is no shifting from doing the things that Jesus said to do, such as loving your neighbor as yourself or even loving your enemies. We shouldn't try to change Christ, because Christ is the same yesterday, today and forever. But we shouldn't expect everything else to stay the same. Jesus was planting Scum of the Earth, and in order for me to fit in, I had to shift my understanding of what a pastor acted like. In Reese's request, I sensed the shift Jesus was asking me to make.

It's hard to know when to shift. Sometimes we're not called to shift; sometimes we're called to stay on course. Knowing when to shift requires us to know the voice of God. Once one of our leaders was giving the announcements during the church service when, all of a sudden from way in the back of the room, a guy came screaming up to the front yelling, "I've got an announcement! I've got an important announcement!" Before I could do anything, he stood at the front of the room and yelled something about the demons that were after him, how he was responsible for the unrest in the Middle East, and how terrified he was. I remember watching the people sitting on the floor up front begin to scoot back away from him like they were in one of those crab-walking relays from elementary school. Things were obviously shifting!

I quietly asked Jesus what to do as I got up from my seat and walked toward him. I had the distinct impression that I should not let one guy's issues derail everything that had been planned for the evening. The thoughts that came to my mind were simply to put my arm around the young man and pray for him—which I did—asking everyone there to pray along with me for his peace.

A couple of women from the singles group I had led at Corona Presbyterian were there visiting that night. They immediately volunteered to take him back into the coffee shop area and pray for him so that we could continue with the service. I remember him shouting to me from the coffee shop area of the building while I gave my message.

"Mike!" he called. "Come on back here! We're having a great discussion!"

"Not right now," I answered into the microphone. "Let me finish my talk and I'll see you later on."

I had a split-second decision to make, but I wasn't alone in the decision. God was there, speaking to me; and his Spirit compelled me to stay the course and finish the sermon for the sake of the other 150 people congregated that night. I like to think that if God had been nudging me to stop in the middle of my message and go attend to this guy back in the coffee shop, I would have done so. But I sensed the opposite.

Through the Holy Spirit I was able to hear God's voice—not, in this case, audibly or even almost audibly, but I felt a definite impression in my soul. We, as God's children, know when to shift and when to stay the course by listening for our Father's voice. That takes training. The place to start to learn God's voice is in the Bible.

Old and New Testaments alike are filled with the commands to hear and listen to God's words as recorded in the Scriptures. Devout Jews in ancient Israel were known to have memorized vast portions of the Old Testament in order to further their relationship with the Lord. Modern ministries such as the Navigators and Walk Thru the Bible have devoted themselves to people's knowing these words of life. This is a life-long process.

But knowing when to shift also involves recognizing God's voice as you encounter it in creation. When looking at a work by our favorite visual artist, we often wonder what the artist was "trying to say" when he or she created it. What does God say to you through sunsets? What does he say to you through a blade of grass? (This may inform you more about his character or personality than which direction you need to go in, but it just might be helpful to know more about the God you are following.) My father-in-law, a scientist and the head of research and development for a large glass and plastics company, would tell me that God made the platypus—an animal with traits of reptiles, mammals and waterfowl—just to play with our tendency to categorize everything!

Sometimes I try to reflect on what God might be telling us by overshadowing cities like Denver with such majestic mountains: about our limitations as human beings, or about how the church we're trying to build fits in the scope of his mission. Sometimes I try to take a step back from Scum of the Earth and think about what God is trying to teach us through the presence of very different people—goths, punks, indie-rockers, ravers and everyone else—in one church. At the very least, the presence of such variety and complexity tells me that God is creative; the flaws that are so evident in the individuals who make up our church and in the church as a whole tell me that God is gracious—that he doesn't demand perfection before committing himself to us.

Given the sophistication of God's creativity and the limitations that are so observable in us, we often need help beyond ourselves to hear God's voice. We are helped in discerning whether God is calling us to shift or stay the course through the advice of trusted leaders, pastors, counselors, friends and family members. They can help us interpret the messages we think we're getting through the Scriptures, our context and the Holy Spirit.

Ultimately, knowing when to shift is more connotation than denotation. It involves shades of meaning—more improvisation than just playing the right notes. You become so skilled at playing the music that you can hear what other notes can fit in to enhance the piece.

God helps us in this. We all know what it is to be thinking one thing while saying another. Maybe we think the next sentence as we utter the first. Perhaps we form a rebuttal even as we are listening to and understanding someone's argument for the first time. For followers of Jesus, there is an ability to carry on a conversation with even several people at once and still, in the back of our minds, carry on a conversation with Jesus. Brother Lawrence of the Resurrection took vows in the 1600s for a life of service and thereafter was a kitchen worker in the priory of a monastery. He practiced this "continual conversation with God" so consistently that he was able to write, in his *Practice of the Presence of God,* that "the time of business does not with me differ from the time of prayer, and in the noise and clatter of my kitchen, while several persons are at the same time calling for different things, I possess God as if I were upon my knees at the blessed sacrament." He became quite famous in his time for giving wise counsel, and was sought after by various leaders for his sound advice. They came to him so that they, too, could shift into the right directions.

Like Brother Lawrence, Frank Laubach (1884-1970), an American missionary to the Philippines, attempted to keep his mind focused on silent conversation with God every minute of the day. In his book *The Game of Minutes* he wrote that our days are filled with moments in which our mind wonders "What next?"

> In these chinks of time, ask Him: "Lord, think Thy thoughts in my mind. What is on Thy mind for me to do now?" When we ask Christ, "What next?" we tune in and give Him a chance to pour His ideas through our enkindled imagination. If we persist, it becomes a habit.

We may already be doing good things, but Jesus knows the better thing. We may think we have just the right thing to say, but Jesus may want us to shift the tone of our voices.

Shifting to follow Jesus in a new direction is not always greeted with applause. Sometimes the call on us to shift meets resistance from people who are either called to something different or are resistant to the same call. There is a kind of love that is present simply because we have grown accustomed to someone. We know what to expect from them and they know what to expect from us. We have become familiar, and we are comfortable together. This kind of love can be present in a church family. But what happens when the pastor goes on for forty-five minutes instead of his typical twenty-five, or the worship team shifts musical genres from praise-rock to a three-piece jazz combo?

Sometimes following Jesus through a shift can make you feel like a Raggedy Ann doll squeezed midway through the rollers of an antique ringer washer. I saw that in a poster; the caption read "The Truth Will Set You Free, But First It Will Make You Miserable." Shifting to follow Jesus will ultimately bring us into a better place, but the path may be rough for a while. The promise that keeps us shifting, however, is that God is with us. God the Father tells us, "I know the plans I have for you." Jesus tells us, "Never will I leave you or forsake you." The still small voice of the Spirit tells us, "This is the way; walk in it."

I remember when Scum was going to make its first move from the Prodigal Coffee House, where we began, to another location. We had scouted out a few church buildings that had been offered to us and had just about settled on one of them. The space was a fairly recent addition onto an old church. Reese was in favor of the move there. We met as a leadership team to finalize the move into the space. Sitting in a circle, each person spoke in turn about liking the place as a new home for our Sunday night service. I was silent. The night before, I had a dream.

We were meeting in that church's building, but something was wrong. The landscape outside was dark and foreboding. Inside the building, I had the feeling of being watched. There was something living inside the walls—a dark, oily, living sludge that listened to our every word. It was really creepy.

Finally, at our meeting, one of the girls asked, "So how do you feel about it, Mike?" I was a bit hesitant to bring up the dream, but if it indeed was a sign for us to shift our plans, I needed to tell them. So I did.

They decided that it was most likely a warning from the Lord that we needed to keep looking. I agreed. It wasn't too long after that the Lord spoke to a man named John Swanger about having us move into his building, called the Tollgate. He had been resistant to the thought at first, as he didn't need a ministry with a name like "Scum of the Earth" to alienate his building's already-difficult neighbors. For John, it was a shift just to come and check us out!

Our eventual move to the Tollgate ended up being a perfect fit. Soon thereafter, John, his wife and their son became an integral part of our Scum community. And a few years later, it was John and his family who moved to Seattle, Washington, to begin the Scum of the Earth Church there. Shifting our plans in order to follow where Jesus leads is really important!

6

Real

The Importance of Being Honest

Who makes you different from anyone else?

*H*ave you ever noticed how pleasant people look when they pray? Their eyes are closed, their hands are folded, their voices are soft. Then there's that concerned tone and the overuse of the word *just.* "Oh God, I *just* want to say, if you could *just* do this . . . and, I'm *just* hoping that . . ."

And so it goes. Everything in the prayer is nice. People are nice when they pray. *I'm* nice when I pray. Why is that? I think I know the answer.

We pray to *God* after all—the Creator, the Omnipotent, the Judge of Everyone, the Big Guy in the Sky. He deserves our respect when we address him verbally. So we are well-mannered. We are polite. We try to hide the rage or apathy that lurks beneath the surface of our words.

I remember reading a book about little kids who, when the sun goes down, are worried that it's never going to come back again. They agonize: *I don't see the sun, therefore it must not exist anymore. I feel that way sometimes about God.* I don't sense God being close by; therefore he must not be present anymore in my life. And yet one of the more common statements from God in Scripture is that he'll be with his people. Jesus said it most starkly: "Be sure of this: I am with you always, even to the end of the age" (Mt 28:20 NLT). He said that shortly before being exalted to heaven—in other words, shortly before what seemed like leaving! In the first chapter of the book of Acts, the disciples are left looking up at a cloud, straining to see him rising into heaven as Jesus is suddenly hidden from their view.

What do we say to people when they feel that God has left them, even though we know that God hasn't? I've been told sometimes, "Well, don't feel that way. If only you had more faith, you would know that God is around." That's a little calloused. That's a little preachy. That's a little self-righteous. Sometimes I've heard things like this: "O you of little faith! Every dark cloud has a silver lining. That's in the Bible somewhere, isn't it?" Or I'll hear people suggest that I take my grief and hide it. "You just need to praise yourself out of despair, brother. Tell God how good he is!"

I don't see that happening in the Scriptures. I see God saying, "I want you to be straightforward with me. I want you to be real with me. Don't come to me with what you think I want to hear. I know how you're really feeling, so tell me."

The fear most Christians have is that they are not good enough for God's family. Each week they are told about the standards they are expected to keep, and each week they are led to believe that the rest of the church is somehow keeping up. This "silence about the struggle" quietly drives people away from churches all over the world.

The people who make up Scum of the Earth Church want to be allowed to struggle. When someone with spiritual authority speaks, week after week, about how things ought to be without acknowledging how badly they themselves have blown it, they are written off as inauthentic. By contrast, one of the highest compliments a pastor can receive is to be told that his or her own difficulty in following Christ has given people in the congregation some hope that they, too, can fail and still keep following Jesus.

One of my favorite movie scenes of all time is from the film *The Apostle*. It's the story about a deeply flawed preacher-evangelist, Sonny. Sonny has had a really bad couple of days. There's been some political maneuvering at church, and as a result, the church is being taken away from him. It's his own fault—he's kind of a rough-and-tumble guy in a lot of ways. There is also the problem of his questionable morality. Sonny has a wandering eye and a weakness for women; as a result, he's just found out that his wife wants a divorce. In addition, Sonny's promiscuity has prompted her to begin an affair of her own with the youth pastor. Sonny finally takes this mess he's made of his life to God in prayer. Since he doesn't want to go home, he travels to his mother's house late at night and goes upstairs to have a chat with God.

> God—somebody, I say *somebody* has taken my wife, has stole my church! That's a temple I built for you. I wanna yell at you, 'cuz I'm mad at you. I . . . cain't . . . take it! Give me a sign or sumthin'. Blow this pain outta me! Give it to me tonight, Lord God Jehovah. If you won't give me back my wife, give me peace. Giveittome, giveittome, giveittome! Give me peace! Give me peace.
>
> I don't know who's been foolin' with me, You or the devil. I don't know. And I won't even bring the human into this. He's just a putz. I'm not even going to bring him into this.

But I'm confused. I'm mad. I love you, Lord, I love you.
But, I'm *mad* at you. I am mad at *you!*

Oh deliver me tonight, Lord. What should I do? Now tell
me! Should I lay hands on myself? What should I do? I know
I'm a sinner and once in a while a womanizer. But I'm your
servant since I was a little boy. You brought me back from
the dead. I am your servant. What should I do? Tell me! I
always call you Jesus, and you always call me Sonny. What
should I do, Jesus? This is Sonny talkin' now . . .

The neighbors call to complain about the noise, but Sonny's
mother simply replies that sometimes Sonny talks to God and sometimes he yells at God. Tonight, she informs them, he's yelling.

Psalm 22, written by King David, has some similarities to Sonny's prayer (in tone at least).

My God, My God, why have you forsaken me?
   Why are you so far from saving me,
   so far from the words of my groaning?
O my God, I cry out by day, but you do not answer,
   by night, and am not silent. (Ps 22:1-2)

Some prayer book, huh? It's extremely real. We don't see David praying with eyes closed, with hands folded, with soft voice
and with a concerned tone. He's yelling at God! He's being honest with God. Have you ever yelled at God? "Well, that wouldn't
be Christian, now would it?" some people might say. But even
Jesus yelled at God, quoting Psalm 22 while he was hanging on
the cross.

The Psalms, of course, were part of Jesus' Bible. He used this
psalm because it accurately depicted how he was feeling. It's like
when you or I go to the Hallmark store, looking for just that right
card to say the words we want to say. Jesus is doing that here. He's

saying that this psalm expresses what he's experiencing. On the cross, Jesus recites the first line of a song and a prayer immediately recognizable to all the onlookers—the religious authorities who arranged for his execution, the followers who were afraid to make their identities known, the passersby on their way to or from Jerusalem, all Jesus' fellow Jews steeped in the ancient writings of their faith, know the opening line: "My God, my God, why have you forsaken me?" And instantly the whole psalm is in everybody's mind.

Can you picture Jesus yelling at God? We need to if we are going to get an accurate picture of the Savior. If that is difficult, think of the most godly person you know, just after something terrible has happened. If that won't do, think of a character from a film, like Jim Carrey in the movie *Bruce Almighty* or Keanu Reeves in *Constantine*. The Old Testament is filled with people being honest with God, lamenting right to his face—Moses, several psalmists, Jeremiah and Isaiah just to name a few. In the book of Revelation, we even see Jesus getting honest and yelling his dissatisfaction with the early church!

I'm a pastor. It's not just my job, it's my gifting. It's what I do. Some pastors are really administrators, some are gifted at teaching, some are tremendous visionaries. I am a pastor, so I talk with people, a lot. I'm with them when they are mad at God—when their fiancée has given back the ring, when their young marriage dissolves into nothing, when their boss hates the fact that they're Christian and makes their days at work miserable, when the lab reports at the doctor's office come back with the worst possible news, when their girlfriend gets the abortion against their appeals. What do you say to the people you love when they are in situations that tear your heart out as their own hearts are being torn? Sometimes I don't say anything; that's often the best that one can do. But often I encourage them to

open up their souls to God with all the hurt and rage that are
there. Yes, it is cathartic, but more than that, they are turning to
a Savior who knows how they feel.

I am poured out like water,
    and all my bones are out of joint.
    My heart has turned to wax;
    it has melted away within me.
My strength is dried up like a potsherd,
    and my tongue sticks to the roof of my mouth;
    you lay me in the dust of death.
Dogs have surrounded me;
    a band of evil men has encircled me,
    they have pierced my hands and my feet.
I can count all my bones;
    people stare and gloat over me.
They divide my garments among them
    and cast lots for my clothing. (Ps 22:14-18)

In Psalm 22, we see a prophetic voice about what was going to
happen to Jesus a millennium later. At the cross we see a lot of
strangely familiar stuff. People are hurling insults at Jesus. People
are casting lots to try and win Jesus' clothing. Jesus complains
about being thirsty. The fact that Jesus references Psalm 22 is no
accident. God is attempting, even while Jesus is on the cross, to
give people one more clue about who he is.

Jesus had told his disciples, "But a time is coming, and has come,
when you will be scattered, each to his own home. You will leave me
all alone. Yet I am not alone, for my Father is with me" (Jn 16:32).
The Father was with him when he was unjustly taken prisoner. The
Father was with him when he was being beaten. The Father was with
him when he was crucified. But in those last three hours, the Father
left him. As soon as that happened, Jesus screamed.

"My God, my God, why have you forsaken me?" This is the only time, in all of the New Testament, where Jesus does not refer to God as Father. There's a distance now between him and the One he loves the most. Why would that happen?

The Scripture says that Jesus allowed himself to be cut off from God so that we would not be cut off from God. When pain roars into our lives, God does not call us to be stoic. He does not expect us to keep stiff upper lips. God expects us to let our true feelings out because he can handle our honest emotions. Jesus was forsaken of God so that we don't have to be. He was cut off from God so that we don't have to be. Jesus said after his resurrection, "I will never leave you nor forsake you." He will never leave us. Never.

But does that mean it will never *feel* like he leaves?

Before Psalm 22 was a prophecy, it was an authentic lament from David to God. In that respect, Jesus is taking upon himself not only the sin of his people but their suffering as well. Is there a spiritual reality operating here? I think so. How else can one explain the ability of Christians through the ages to bear up—and keep loving—in some of the most horrible scenarios imaginable? Jesus bears our pain.

Several years ago my sister-in-law walked into her seventeen-year-old son's bedroom one morning to find that he had died in his sleep of a heart arrhythmia. The grief was overwhelming. My wife flew out immediately to be with her sister and brother-in-law, and hardly ever left her sister's side. The death of a child can wreck marriages, drag people into substance abuse, even lead some to commit suicide. But my wife's sister, Helen, and her husband, Bill, knew that God had not forsaken them. They knew that Jesus grieved with them. They were honest about their suffering. And they found hope for each day in the Lord. To this day, my sister-in-law prays every morning words from Psalm 118:

"This is the day the LORD has made. I will rejoice and be glad in
it." Bill has begun an event called Dad's Day, monthly breakfasts
which strengthen the bonds between fathers and their children.
The idea has caught on, and now there are hundreds of Dad's Day
breakfasts taking place every month.

I can't think of an anguish more intense than the death of one's
own child. I was with a young couple at Scum who went through
the miscarriage of their first pregnancy. They likened the experience with God to sitting on their father's lap while pounding on
his chest. They were in agony, but they had a place to go for as
much comfort as they could receive.

At the end of Psalm 22, there's a note of triumph.

> The poor will eat and be satisfied;
>   they who seek the LORD will praise him—
>   may your hearts live forever!
> All the ends of the earth
>   will remember and turn to the LORD,
>   and all the families of the nations
>   will bow down before him,
> for dominion belongs to the LORD
>   and he rules over the nations.
> All the rich of the earth will feast and worship;
>   all who go down to the dust will kneel before him—
>   those who cannot keep themselves alive.
> Posterity will serve him;
>   future generations will be told about the Lord.
> They will proclaim his righteousness
>   to a people yet unborn—
>   for he has done it.

By referencing Psalm 22, Jesus chose to complain vigorously
about his suffering. But the psalm also looks beyond the anguish

to express faith. Jesus knew how the psalm ended, even there on the cross, and he held on to God. He was the founding member of a special club: *Those Who Hang On.* "In spite of the fact that I am separated from God," they cry, "I will not stop hoping."

We all have or will have the opportunity to become members of Those Who Hang On. To be sure, we will never have to go through all that Jesus did in being forsaken of God (even though sometimes it can feel like that). But we will be tempted to stop being honest, to give up, to quit sitting on his lap, to quit pounding on his chest, to quit rejoicing in the new day he has made. And in that day, we will be invited into the ranks of Those Who Hang On. And if we decline that invitation, we will cease to be real—not just in our relationship with God but in our relationships with others.

Too often Christians feel that they have to put on a self-sufficient facade in order to impress those with whom they're talking about Jesus. That is no way to start a relationship, because love takes time and being real means we share our weaknesses as well as our strengths. When we are real with non-Christians, our faith becomes real as well.

But even *becoming* real takes time. In *The Velveteen Rabbit,* a stuffed toy called the Skin Horse is telling Rabbit what it takes to be real:

> It doesn't happen all at once like being wound up, but bit by bit. It doesn't happen all at once. You become. It takes a long time. That's why it doesn't often happen to people who break easily, or who have sharp edges, or who have to be carefully kept. Generally, by the time you are real, most of your hair has been loved off, and your eyes drop out and you get loose in the joints and very shabby. But these things don't matter at all because once you are real you can't be ugly, except to people who don't understand.

A young man and a young woman fall in love and head toward
marriage. There's a lot that they don't know about each other
initially. At some point, the less-than-beautiful truths about each
other have to come out into the open. What if one person refused
to let those imperfect realities see the light of day? The relationship would become a sham, a mere illusion of what it ought to
have been. Over time, as opposed to loving each other more, the
couple would slowly drift apart until there was no actual relationship at all—whether they became married or not.

Conversely, what about the young couple who are honest with
each other? As less-than-beautiful truths emerge, they talk about
them. They work out the problems these imperfections cause.
Perhaps, out of love for one another, they even postpone the wedding until they deal with things honestly. They get real and then
commit to each other in holy matrimony. By the time this couple
is old and worn with their hair falling out, their eyesight fading
and their joints getting loose, they have experienced what it means
to be genuinely in love.

The non-Christians I know are looking for what is real. In a
culture where spouses split apart more often than they hang on,
the testimony of a couple that has honestly loved each other
through the less-than-beautiful times is inspiring. As we become
real with people, they will eventually see beauty in us, and they
themselves become real to us.

When we're real with God, he shows us his love and we see
him for who he really is: beautiful, glorious, perfect, merciful,
compassionate and true. Honest to God, he does.

7

Broken

Christ's Mosaic

We are in rags, we are brutally treated, we are homeless.

$\mathcal{H}$aving a church for the "left-out and the right-brained" makes for a very dangerous combination. One of the bumper sticker ideas an artist at Scum came up with says, "Scum of the Earth: Our Congregation Could Kick Your Congregation's Ass."

I feel the same way about that sticker as some parents do about their "My Kid Could Take Your Honor Student" stickers. Ours is a church full of people who have been hurt throughout their lives. They have every defense up. That reality makes things difficult for people who want to offer the love of Christ to them.

Another bumper sticker reads, "Scum of the Earth: Just When You Thought It Was Safe to Go to Church." Our church is not for people who are faint at heart. We have a meal every Sunday, smack-dab in the middle of the worship time. More often than not, the long line of people waiting to get food is made up of regular attenders and homeless people, newcomers plus other people who are coming just for the free food. We have officially designated our smokers as the greeters since they are already out front. "Don't scare people," I plead. "Smile and say hello. Offer them a cigarette." Sometimes I'll drive up on a Sunday before service and see a motley group of people waiting to get in. I dodge into the side door because I've got so much on my mind right then—the sermon, the communion, wondering how the band is doing, wondering if the chairs are being set up. I just can't take one more weight on my scale. Sometimes going to church is scary, even for me.

Church does not feel safe when the walls are precarious. I thank God that the foundation is strong, but how does one deal with broken bricks? We need to go to the Scriptures to see how Jesus dealt with the broken.

"When Jesus had again crossed over by boat to the other side of the lake," Mark 5:21 says, "a large crowd gathered around him while he was by the lake. Then one of the synagogue rulers, named Jairus, came there. Seeing Jesus, he fell at his feet and pleaded earnestly with him, 'My little daughter is dying. Please come and put your hands on her so that she will be healed and live.' So Jesus went with him."

Jesus had just come from healing a demoniac. Back on the far side of the lake, Jesus had walked toward a guy with thousands of demons inside of him and set him free by throwing the demons into a herd of pigs. The pigs had gone rushing down a hill, committing suicide. After Jesus performed this amazing miracle, the people of that region said something like, "Please leave us! You are bad for business! We can't take another loss like that; those pigs were our livelihood!" Their business interests may have been a good excuse to cover up their real fear of Jesus' great power. In any case, Jesus had just come from complete rejection by a whole region of people on the other side of the lake. Who knows what

Jesus had in mind? Maybe he wanted to get a little rest and relaxation at some friend's house, but as soon as he stepped off the boat he was interrupted by Jairus.

Here's a guy who is wealthy by the standards of the culture. He is important, a synagogue ruler. He is probably a nice guy. Not one of the Pharisees, he is actually a man of the people, and yet he is one of the upper crust. Among the congregations of our churches, he'd be one of the "big tithers." He's got all the things that the culture has to offer, but he's broken: his daughter is dying.

In the Greek the word is *eschatos* (from which we get our word *eschatology,* the study of the end times). Jairus says, essentially, "My daughter is in her last days. She is at death's door." He comes broken to Jesus and pleads, "Please come and put your hands on her so that she will live."

Jesus goes with him. As simple as that. But the passage goes on.

> A large crowd followed and pressed around him. And a woman was there who had been subject to bleeding for twelve years. She had suffered a great deal under the care of many doctors and had spent all she had, yet instead of getting better she grew worse. When she heard about Jesus, she came up behind him in the crowd and touched his cloak, because she thought, "If I just touch his clothes, I will be healed." Immediately her bleeding stopped and she felt in her body that she was freed from her suffering. (Mark 5:24-29)

This is not proper Hebrew form for approaching God. It is not even proper for her, as a woman, to accost a male teacher in this way. This is a strange occurrence in the life of Jesus.

> At once Jesus realized that power had gone out from him. He turned around in the crowd and asked, "Who touched my clothes?"

"You see the people crowding against you," his disciples answered, "and yet you can ask, 'Who touched me?' "

But Jesus kept looking around to see who had done it. Then the woman, knowing what had happened to her, came and fell at his feet and, trembling with fear, told him the whole truth. (Mk 5:30-33)

Representatives of Christ will deal with all kinds of things like this. In our churches and with the people we meet in our daily lives, we deal with unexpected death and illness and, often, financial hardship. We know couples dealing with the heartbreak of infertility. We are friends with couples that have divorced, damaging themselves and their children. I have a friend who is seventy-eight years old and worries about the time he'll call his wife and she won't respond; he's afraid to face "an end to decades of conversation." We know people who are addicted to other people or to sex, drugs or alcohol. Sometimes we meet people who are addicted to church—the form, not the substance. These people act religious but reject the power that could make them godly (2 Tim 3:5 NLT). As a result, it may be among the worst of addictions. The cure is right there in front of them, but they can't see it and insist that God says they are fine.

Usually broken people don't turn to the church until everything else has failed them. Then church wants to take its time and review the situation and present it to a board for approval. Meanwhile, these folks are frightened and clueless about what to do next. People's frustration with organized Christianity is understandable. As followers of Jesus we must expect to be overwhelmed, to be interrupted, to be drained and to be misunderstood.

A majority of the people I deal with on a regular basis at Scum are from broken homes. Their parents are divorced or their dad was never around—or when he was around, he was so unavailable it wasn't even funny. I have a congregation that desperately needs a father figure, and I'm one of the few guys there over fifty. But people have this strange "Go away—come closer" thing. "I need you," they seem to suggest, "but I can't listen to what you're saying." "Oh please, Mike, comfort me; but I can't hear the hard word from you. Just like my dad, you'll probably hurt me."

I have dealt with at least four sexual molestation accusations within the congregation in the short life of Scum of the Earth. It is strange that the number would be this large, but I think it's related to the widespread breakdown of people's family structure. People at Scum tend to travel in packs. They go to the Breakfast King Diner, they go to a movie, they go to the Sixteenth Street Mall, they go to a concert in these packs. Then late at night, when everything else is done, they go back to someone's apartment, lie all over the floor and watch a movie, using each other as body pillows. Then some girl wakes up at three in the morning being kissed and such by the guy that she's been using as a body pillow all night.

This terrible invasion of her space and privacy is uncalled for, but given what has transpired throughout the night, really it isn't all that surprising. I talk to the guy involved and he tells me, "She was sending me signals all night like she wanted to make out." I try to tell him that he can't take that step without her permission. I ask the girl if she wants to talk to the police; so far, every girl has said no. I suggest that she seek counseling and require that he see a counselor. I have to clean up the mess and try to teach proper boundaries at the same time.

A girl was having nightmares about going under anesthetic for a minor surgery the following week. She was terrified that she wouldn't wake up, that she was going to die during surgery. Her counselor, my wife and I guessed it was the guilt of an abortion that was causing these dreams. She's not alone; there are a number of people at Scum who have had abortions. In some cases the abortion has been avoided, and that has been glorious. I wish I could say that every time. When young Christian men and women agree to abort their babies, there are broken pieces of their hearts to pick up; it's gut-wrenching to be the one to love them.

The most overwhelming thing that happened to me in a very long time was during a time period when I was trying to avoid any extra pressure. The burdens of ministry were piling up. I felt unable to do anything but the bare minimum. There were probably stress-cracks under my scalp from the tension in my head. Then came the situation to end all situations. "There's a homeless guy looking for an ordained pastor, and you're the only one we know that is ordained."

I asked, "Has he been around Scum often?"

"No."

"I'll tell you what then, you deal with it. I'm too busy right now and I can't handle it."

But eventually I had to walk through the foyer, and the guy spotted me. He had the wild-eyes look. His hair was everywhere. He was dirty. He asked me, "Are you the ordained pastor? I've got to talk to an ordained pastor."

At that point I felt the rather loud voice of Jesus saying, "You can't get out of this now, Mike." And so I took the man back to a room in the church. While we were back there, he began to pre-amble a confession; he wanted to make sure that he would not be legally prosecuted for what he was about to confess. I didn't even know the guy's last name, and he obviously didn't have an address to send the police to. So I assured him that I wouldn't turn him in; that he could count on pastoral confidentiality. Then he told me: he had murdered another homeless man that week and couldn't get the man's face out of his mind.

And I thought I was overwhelmed before! I gathered my wits

and proceeded to talk about Jesus and his forgiveness, but the man just couldn't accept that Jesus would forgive him for what he had done. Inside, he wanted to pay for his sin. I encouraged him to turn himself in to the police, but assured him that I wouldn't. We prayed together.

After the man left the building, I walked out of that room feeling the way it feels after you hear a really loud noise and you can't hear much else for a while afterward. I was thinking Jesus had the potential to be overwhelmed all the time. How did Jesus handle such things?

Jesus did everything in obedience to his Father. He didn't say anything the Father didn't say, and he didn't do anything the Father didn't do. The way Jesus speaks of obedience to God isn't just about personal piety—watching our mouths and not watching porn, or whatever. It's also about encountering broken people—something inevitable in a broken world and unavoidable to people who follow the Savior of the broken—and then looking to God to see how he responds. Broken people didn't undo Jesus because Jesus kept God in view. That may sound convenient—he was, after all, Jesus. We must keep in mind the truth that, in addition to dying for us, Jesus *lived* for us. We are to mimic the manner in which he was obedient to his Father. The way Jesus speaks of obedience is a reminder that we're not alone in our encounters with broken people. God was with Jesus, and God has promised to be with us. We can't handle such things by ourselves when they inevitably come up. We have to go to Jesus with them.

Jesus has also promised to respond to the broken who turn to him; we have the privilege of accompanying God in his response. To interact meaningfully with broken people, of course, we have to be prepared to be interrupted by them. A young man I met at a local night club walked around with the weight of the world on his shoulders, as though there were a dark cloud following him.

He came to church the week after I met him and asked if I could pray for him. I asked him what his prayer request was.

"Well, I have been involved in the occult for eight years. I have four demons living inside of me, and I need you to get them out."

I was stunned, to say the least. "Go on upstairs and wait for me," I told him. There was no way I was going to try and deal with this all by myself. I went to find a few more people that I could trust to pray for this guy. It was at times like these that I was thankful for my experience in a charismatic church! I scanned the young Scum congregation for people I knew who had been at least partially brought up in such churches. Soon Reese, Ruth, Melanie and I were walking up the stairs. While we were praying, by the grace of God, four demons came out.

I am a bit reluctant to offer the details of the deliverance session we participated in that night. It wasn't that dramatic. The man's head did not turn around 360 degrees and he did not vomit out green slime. That night, God used each one of us to hear different promptings from the Spirit, speak to the young man firmly but kindly, and call out different evil spirits. It was a community effort, and after it was all over, we prayed with him to acknowledge Jesus as Lord and be filled with the Holy Spirit, all to the glory of the Father.

I have been involved in a few of these at Scum of the Earth Church and elsewhere. Each is different. Suffice it to say that a lot of listening to the Holy Spirit is involved. Jesus provided templates for this kind of ministry himself in the Gospels and through the apostles in the book of Acts. My point here is not about exorcism, but about our having to be open to interruptions ordained by God—in this case, a young man who desperately needed freedom from demonic spirits.

The next week he was in church with us again. The black band T-shirt he wore had a half-naked woman on the front, reclining with her feet up near his neck. His tattoos and piercing were clearly visible. But it was his stance that struck me. During the singing, his head was tilted back, with his face toward the ceiling. His eyes were closed, and he was singing with his whole voice, lifting his hands and praising God. That is a scene that I will never forget. We arranged to have him live in a room at an Assemblies of God church downtown.

Not long after his conversion he told me that he was in love with a homeless girl who was Wiccan. They asked me to perform a wedding ceremony for them. He had no permanent place to live, and the girl had two children from two other men. I said, "I don't know. Can you ask anyone else?" He told me that they had asked a Wiccan priestess to do the ceremony, but something was wrong with the seasons and the moon, so she wasn't able to do it. I thanked them for being so honest and for making me their second choice, but I told them that there was no way my Boss would let me do it. They found another pastor to marry them and then promptly left the state for the Pacific Northwest.

Months later a car pulled right up next to me and parked on Colfax. Who could it be but this couple and one of their kids! "Hi, we're here!" they shouted through the open window.

"Where are you going to stay?" I asked.

"I don't know. In the car?" they responded.

Everything I had planned for the day had to come to a grinding halt. We had to find them a hotel and then a place to live. We took them to a ministry, Joshua Station, that helps get street families back on their feet—a kind of halfway house. In the middle of this, the young woman began the process of coming to Christ.

Back then we had this Maundy Thursday movie night. On the Thursday before Easter we decided to show the Video-Bible version of the life of Jesus—the Gospel of Matthew abridged down to about two hours. I had gone to pick them up so that they were both there for the movie. After the movie night I was taking them back to where they were living, when the Wiccan girl spoke up. "Mike, I have a question."

"What is it?" I asked.

"Something I didn't quite get. You know that part in the movie where Jesus is walking with his disciples, and they ask him what should you do when somebody sins against you, and Jesus says you should go and talk to that person just to resolve it, and if that person doesn't listen then you should go get somebody else to come with you, and then they all talk, and if that doesn't work you bring them to the whole church, and if that doesn't work then you treat them like you would treat a tax collector or a sinner?"

"Yeah, I remember that part. Matthew 18."

"Well, isn't that who Jesus' friends were—the tax collectors and sinners?"

"Ummm . . ."

This little Wiccan girl was schooling the pastor! Matthew was a tax collector himself! A passage that so often is used as an excuse to stop caring for someone frustrating or annoying became, in the naive observations of this pre-Christian homeless woman, a reminder of God's loving concern. She came to Christ shortly thereafter.

The couple hung around through all sorts of ups and downs for a while after that. They had another baby, and then they disappeared again to the Northwest.

Sometime later a couple of friends and I had just come back from a concert and were hanging out at my house. It had been a wonderful evening; Christian recording artist Phil Keaggy had just presented our departing worship leader, Deva, with a guitar from Scum as a goodbye present. At about 11:30 my cell phone rang. I warned my son: "Don't answer the cell phone at 11:30! Don't do it!"

"Why, Dad? It's for you."

It was the husband calling from the Pacific Northwest. "Mike, you've got to help me. My wife's in jail." It turns out that some years earlier, they had been caught swimming in a river on someone's private property. The warrant for her arrest in the state was still outstanding, and when the police found out that they had come back, they picked her up. There was no holding facility in the little town where they were, so the police were going to take her two-and-a-half hours away to a holding facility at the county seat, and then transfer her some ten hours away to some other kind of jail. The husband, left alone with two of their kids (the third was now with his father), asked me for help. "We've got this much money raised for her bail, and we can't get the rest."

"It's almost midnight! What do you want me to do?" I pled, but then I gave in. One of the guys from the church staff was at my house with us; we went to five different places in Denver looking for some way to wire money to a grocery store in a tiny town in the Northwest. The store manager there was staying open just so he could receive the money for these people. By 1:30 a.m. we were finished, and she was able to go home with her family.

As a follower of Jesus you have to do what you have to do, even if that means being interrupted. Our caring for people is going to cost us something. In many cases it will drain us of our energy. We are going to be depleted if we follow Christ.

There has been no person who has drained me as much as a young man at Scum we called Gothic Sean. Obsessive-compulsive, slightly paranoid and with a severe case of ADHD, he didn't really fit into a normal work-a-day world. He lived on assistance from the federal government because he couldn't hold a "normal" job. With all his free time, he became the self-styled evangelist for the Capitol Hill area of Denver, where we do most of our ministry. We called him Gothic Sean because he was definitely a goth—the music, the dark clothes, the fishnet sleeves, the black boots, all of it. But he was known pretty much as the Jesus freak of the community in which he operated, which was wonderful.

Eventually, though, things took a bad turn for him. He had a series of unfortunate relationships that left him feeling very broken. He decided to take solace in alcohol, but it went out of control. One time during our lunch together he was "talking" to me while lying on the bench under the table; he was too hung over to sit up. It looked like I was having lunch with nobody. It felt like the Holy Spirit told me he was going to die if he kept up what he was doing.

During this period he began to drink so much that he would forget to eat, and he became malnourished. In the span of three months he was in the emergency room ten times. His apartment was getting terribly trashed and smelled of rotting food. We sent people from Scum twice to clean out his apartment so he wouldn't be evicted. And still I was ending up at the hospital a few times a month.

Gothic Sean would call me sometimes a dozen times a week. I gave him a special ringtone on my phone so that I would know it was him. I wouldn't answer. I felt that God said, "You don't have to answer the phone every time he calls. Just listen to the messages, delete them and then get back to him." I would call him back twice a week—if he was not at the hospital.

The last time he tried to quit drinking, he was sober for several days when he had what is called a delirium tremens flashback. He went crazy and started seeing things—things like a guy with his head cut off and people melting like wax. It was so frightening to him that he broke out the window of his apartment and cut his arms up. The glass fell down and scratched up the new car of one of the other tenants (another phone call that I had to deal with). Having broken out of his window, he went running out into

Capitol Hill, where he was picked up and taken into the medical ICU and then sent into detox. After that he went to the psych ward where I was able to visit him. There, he slowly but surely got better as he began to kick his addiction. But there were many more episodes to come.

I pleaded with the staff at Scum, "Please come around Gothic Sean. He is going to die if we don't do something now. I need your help. I am drained. The power has gone out of me and I need to be replenished. Please, give me a breather." When some people started to protest, I just stopped. I hardly ever get this way with my staff, but I felt filled with a kind of righteous indignation. "Listen! Jesus said that whatever you do for the least of these my brothers you've done to me. You're not doing this for Gothic Sean, you're doing this for Jesus Christ." And with that, they did.

Following Jesus means getting drained sometimes. It also often means being misunderstood. Walt, at age thirty (a little older than the average guy at Scum), used to stay in the background talking to a select group of people. I later found out that he had been their youth pastor once upon a time, but since the deconstruction of that youth group, he had gone through a divorce. His wife may have had good reasons for leaving him, but it just devastated Walt. He had gone through bankruptcy; his business had crumbled. He had contracted prostate cancer. This young man was a mess; he was about as broken as they come.

He was living with some of his former youth group kids. As a former youth pastor, I can't think of anything more humiliating than going back to the kids you led in high school and saying, "I need your help. I need a place to live." To numb the pain he had begun drinking. Sometimes it was the physical pain of the cancer he was trying to numb, sometimes it wasn't. He didn't have insurance, and as I got to know him I tried to convince him to go to clinics. We had long talks, but his life was just in shambles. He even began stealing, we think, from the guys he was living with; they came to me and said, "The camera I got from my parents is missing" or "My music equipment wasn't missing until Walt came to live with us." And so I had to try and confront him with that. As I tried to confront him he began to retreat from me.

One time Walt had outstayed all of his welcomes, so I let him stay in the Tollgate, which we were renting for our church services. I wasn't really allowed to do anything like that, but the guy had no other place to go so I let him stay there for a couple nights. "Just clean up around here. I'll tell them you're our live-in janitor, and I think we can get away with it." A few days later, the two of us were supposed to have a meeting in the morning. He didn't show up. I thought I should go over to the Tollgate and see what was going on.

The door was locked. When I opened it the heat was incredible. It must have been at least ninety degrees in there. I went upstairs and found Walt passed out on the floor with an empty bottle of vodka. I didn't know what to do. I woke him up and said, "What are you doing? You can't do this, this is not our building! I took a risk in bringing you here." And so I had to kick him out. He left, and I had no idea where he went.

Later I learned that Walt was up in Montana working for his dad's friend, a believer who had been an alcoholic himself. This man had been through a twelve-step program and was shepherding Walt in ways that I never could have.

Walt was living in the trailer behind the guy's house. One morning he came in to have breakfast, and then he went out on the front porch to wait for the guy to pull his car around. He died on the front steps, just like that. His heart just stopped at thirty years old. I went to the funeral and even spoke there; it was hard because we had reached that stage in our relationship where we weren't even friends. I felt like I had failed Walt. I wish I had done more to contact him in Montana, but I hadn't.

One of God's great graces to me came at the time of Walt's death, in the person of his employer. This dear, older Christian man had known about the distance between Walt and me. While he was looking through some of the papers on Walt's desk, he came across a letter Walt was in the process of writing to me. In it, Walt was asking my forgiveness for the things he had done and the way he had ignored me. It brought peace to my soul.

Back at Scum of the Earth, we got Walt's former youth group kids together and put on a memorial service. The place was packed out; you could not move inside the Tollgate because of the crowd. I invited whoever wanted to say anything about Walt to come forward and share with us. I sat there and listened in awe. Walt had loved these people when nobody else would love them; he had believed in them when nobody else thought they had a chance. It was the single most powerful service I have been to of any kind in my entire life. It was as if Jesus were making this mosaic for me; every little story contributed to this full-blown image of Walt, how God had intended him to be, how God had used him, and how Walt had been for so much of his life. It was beautiful.

There is a picture of Christ from Hagia Sophia, the once great Greek Orthodox Cathedral in Istanbul, Turkey. *Christ Pantocrator* is a mosaic composed of thousands of little tiny pieces of glass and stone that go together to make a complete picture. In the 1400s, the great edifice that housed *Christ Pantocrator* became a mosque. Today, Hagia Sophia is a museum. Down at the bottom of the picture, the years have worn the mosaic away. There are little imperfections in it here and there. I'm sure that it looked terrific eight hundred years ago, but I like it better now. Not only is the picture itself broken up, but it is now smack-dab in the middle of a non-Christian context. That is what I get out of following Christ into brokenness. It means to be overwhelmed, interrupted, drained and misunderstood in a world that desperately needs to hear who Jesus really is. Christians are all wounded healers— wandering sheep who are now shepherds. We were fish who are now fishermen and fisherwomen. We are the cracked, broken and chipped bricks of the house of God that now form a cathedral— little shards of tile and glass that fit into a larger mosaic.

8
Loss

Blessed Endurance

To this very hour we go hungry and thirsty.

I have nostalgic memories about the first group of young adults that met in our living room to dream up and design what became Scum of the Earth Church. I think that both my wife and I had hopes that we would see people grow up, get jobs—that some would get married and we'd see their babies. But things rarely work out the way we imagine they will.

The great part of ministering to young adults is helping them to make wise choices for some of the biggest decisions in their lives. The difficult part is watching them make poor choices and then enduring the consequences. The group that started Scum was unique in that even though they were skeptical about the church as a whole, they were people with vision. They had a passion for what they were creating and the people it would reach. I think it's the same way with any group that begins just about anything. Risk-takers are of a different breed, and they tend to get a little bored when stuff goes smoothly. Some church-planter friends told me, at the time, to look around my living room and to realize that most of the people present there would not be with us in five years. I did not want to believe my friends; I thought we could be different. But they were right.

Our expectations are normally long-term. I believe there's something inside each of us that longs for heaven. The writer of Ecclesiastes suggests as much, that God himself has "set eternity in the hearts of men." And yet, as he goes on to say, "They cannot fathom what God has done from beginning to end" (Eccles 3:11). The longing for longevity is deep within us, but it is not our present reality. People graduate from college and then move. People get married and move. People have children and move. People get restless and move. Sometimes people die. Living on this side of eternity means dealing with loss.

For the person moving on, very often, things feel great. He or she has entered a new phase of life. But for the people left behind, it can feel devastating. I can appreciate that; if I were changing universities and everyone was glad that I was going, that would feel wrong to me. It's appropriate that we mourn when people leave. It shows that the people who are leaving have played a significant role in our lives and that we will miss them.

When I was doing singles ministry at my former church, three bachelors were the ringleaders. They planned events and were the de facto escorts for various weddings. They were confidants for several women. Things changed drastically when all three guys became engaged to women outside the group. There was a sadness in the people who were left in the singles group. What were they going to do with their time now that the event planners were no longer planning events? How were they going to get much-needed and proper attention now that these guys, who had been like brothers to them, were engaged and ultimately would be married?

I've felt a similar loss at times. When Five Iron Frenzy called it quits, Reese got to work on forming a new band. I had sensed a distance growing between us even while FIF was on its intentionally ironic "Winners Never Quit" tour. In the band's absence I had been exercising more and more authority at Scum and invariably made decisions Reese didn't agree with. Meanwhile, his engagement to a lovely girl had gone awry, and he was looking for God's will in both his personal and vocational life.

I learned later from Reese that he had been looking at the growth at Scum of the Earth and concluded that I needed either for him to be around much more than he had been, or for someone to replace him totally. He knew he couldn't commit to all that Scum required, and he felt I would never replace him if he stuck around, even in a limited capacity. So he decided to move to California to record a new project. He said he didn't know when he'd be back in Denver.

I had never envisioned Reese's departure. His fingerprints were all over the church, and I had little confidence in my ability to relate to a younger generation without him. It felt like God was asking me to harvest wheat with one hand.

Prior to Reese's leaving, the greatest loss by far I had experienced was the death of my mother when I was twelve years old, in middle school. The four years after she died and before my father remarried were emotionally desolate. Even recently I have wondered how different my life would be if she had lived longer. When someone important in your life dies, a part of you dies with them. Different people call different things, good things, out of us. If my mother had lived longer, I think I would have been more disciplined about writing this book; she was the parent who pressed me on studying and doing my homework! Similarly, I have not always been the best at relating to women, an inability my wife attributes to the absence of a mom for those critical years. The Lord has helped me over the years, of course, through my wife, my stepmother and other women in the church. But I think one of the pieces we miss when people leave us is that particular part of ourselves they actualized which no one else could. We feel we were better people when he or she was around; and now, in the absence of that person, we are left to face the worst in ourselves alone.

Loss reveals what we're made of. Psychologist Larry Crabb has said that in order to reveal our hearts, our minds must be offended. Loss offends us. My friend Steve Garcia likens the effects of loss to when a man pans for gold. The motion of the shaking allows him to separate the gravel and the rocks from the gold that he's after. Loss does that for us. It's one way that God takes the gravel out of our hearts, leaving the gold. It is contrary to our expectations, so our true characters are revealed.

How was I to react to Roper's leaving Scum? I was hurt; could I have attacked him, questioned his loyalty to the church he helped begin, questioned his loyalty to me, even to God? Maybe, but it never occurred to me. Perhaps there are benefits to being twenty years older than your co-pastor! If there had been jealousy, anger or resentment inside of me toward Reese when he left, it would have come out, and God would have dealt with me in it. But Reese's and my relationship would have suffered badly. Fortunately, Reese and I parted on good terms and stayed in contact. I recommended him for a job as the young adult ministry director at a friend's church. I was the oldest groomsman at his wedding.

As Christians, we have to learn to let people go into the grace and care of God. We need to bless them in their leaving as much as we blessed them in their arriving. Being a pastor, I tend to see people as God's sheep. He may have me take care of one of his lambs in my sheepfold for a given period of time, for a specific purpose; but when that purpose has been accomplished, the Good Shepherd may move his lamb to a different sheepfold. I have to be OK with that, or risk a stern correction from my employer, the Great Shepherd.

Romantic loss can be even more devastating to a person than the loss of a friend. The end of a romantic relationship can reveal more about a person than he or she ever wished or imagined. I've seen intelligent and mature people become stalkers. I've seen easygoing folks become bitter and angry. Loss reveals the character traits we'd hidden so well when the romantic relationship began.

I liken this process to my experience in the steel mill: scrap metal is placed into a furnace (picture a gigantic pot lined with bricks). The lid comes down hydraulically, and then three immense electrodes descend through three holes in the lid. Sixty million volts of electricity (with 40,000 amps) arcing between the electrodes melt the metal. What fireworks! The sound is deafening. The building shakes. Sounds like romance, right?

As the contents of the furnace melt, the impurities present in the scrap metal rise to the top. Ugly stuff. So steelworkers tap the furnace from the bottom, where the good steel is. The bad stuff gets dumped into a sand pit to cool, and from there the "slag" is hauled away.

Loss turns up the heat in our souls so that God can get rid of the slag that's inside of us. I watched this happen when Reese's fiancée broke off their wedding plans without explaining why. The slag that was in Reese's heart surprised him, and as he did about a lot of what was going on in his life, he wrote a song about it, called "Enamel."

> Here's another song
> With the four oldest chords in history
> I guess I lost all ambition
> Turning left on misery

I could have made it better
But the feelings just aren't there
My heart is cold and black
But I just don't think I care
So here's to me saying, "fare-thee-well"
And when you hear this song I hope it hurts like hell

Enamel is stretched too thin
You're beautiful,
But not beneath your skin

The phone lines down in Mexico
Are slow and maybe tired
I guess all your devotion
Got lost inside the wires
Well I hope you cannot sleep
And I hope you cannot smile
And I hope that you are burdened with
Your guilt for quite a while,
I hope you fall in love
But I hope your plans are thwarted,
And I hope that now you're back
It's because you were deported

Enamel is stretched too thin
You're beautiful,
But not beneath your skin
Enamel, like insect shells
So hollow, like your wedding bells

Can you say, "angry lyrics"? You're lucky you didn't hear the
first draft! It was ugly stuff on a very ugly day. Reese made it
through that dark time. It was difficult, but he emerged a more
virtuous man. God is faithful, and Reese ended up marrying an

amazing, godly woman named Amy. She really was the right one for him—and the losses in his life had prepared him for her.

In this life we are guaranteed nothing, and if we take Jesus as our model—whose friends scattered right at the moment of his greatest need—then it's reasonable to presume that some of us may have to walk the path of losing everything. In a very basic way, we just need to appreciate what is happening in the present. For now I have these friends. Today I am in this group of believers at this particular church. It is only for a span of time in my life that I will be married. One of us will likely die before the other, and in a culture where divorce is so widespread, we might be foolish to suppose that it will be death that finally separates us. Those of us that have children are not guaranteed that our babies will outlive us. Only one guarantee stands: the inexplicable power of God to comfort us during affliction, for even when everybody forsakes, Jesus never leaves us. We always have the presence of God.

I think that sometimes God grants us spiritual amnesia. It's really a blessing to have certain memories fade. I remember moving from my hometown of Toledo, Ohio, to Denver, Colorado. At that point I had wonderful friendships, some of which were twenty years deep. I had been single for a quarter century while I lived in Ohio, and after that I was newly married with no children, so a lot of my time was given to hanging out with friends and other couples. I left Ohio with a car full of children, which meant that I was also leaving friendships that would never be replaced. People with children have less time for adult friendships; as time goes by, their need for friends is supplanted by the family's needs.

For the first couple of years in Denver, I ached for our old friends. But the longer we lived in Denver, the more fuzzy our memories became, and the more distant our friends remained. There was a blessedness in that amnesia. I stopped comparing my new friends to my old friends. I was able to enjoy my new friends much more.

As I've gotten even older, there are other losses that I've begun to endure. I distinctly remember the summer that I had to give up playing basketball. The cartilage in my knees had begun wearing down, and the pain I was feeling after each workout was greater than the pleasure that I received from playing. And so I had to give it up. I lost the ability to play basketball.

My father-in-law, Josef Francel, died of Alzheimer's Disease. The losses endured by a person with Alzheimer's are brutal. He had been a genius before the disease took his memories. He had been born in what is now the Czech Republic and survived the Nazi occupation of his homeland. He had been the president of the student body at the University of Brno when the Communists were taking over. Outspoken against the takeover, he had been taken captive, tortured and marked for death. Miraculously, he had escaped to Western Europe in 1948 and eventually made it to the United States. He had received a doctorate in chemical engineering from MIT. He had learned five languages and registered over 180 patents. Watching this great man lose everything except for the love of his family and his love for God was one of the most humbling things I have ever seen. The priest at his funeral read this prayer by St. Ignatius Loyola (1491-1556):

> Lord Jesus Christ, take away my freedom, my memory, my understanding, and my will. All that I have and cherish you have given me. I surrender it all to be guided by your will. Your love and your grace are wealth enough for me. Give me these, Lord Jesus. I ask for nothing more. Amen.

Loss is a severe mercy. A friend of mine, Les Avery, says that the mark of adulthood is the ability to endure a series of losses. Loss changes us. If we respond correctly, it changes us for the better. I've had to rethink who I am in light of what remains after each loss. God is paring me down; one day I will have nothing left, except for my relationship with him. Each loss prepares us in part for that eventuality. We revisit the promises of God and realize just how good "pretty good" can be.

Young adults don't deal with death very often, and when it comes it hits hard. Gothic Sean died a tragic death, literally freezing to death one night behind a restaurant in Boulder, Colorado. My eulogy for him was delivered to a congregation of people who were not accustomed to the reality of such permanent, final loss.

◆   ◆   ◆

"Maybe it's appropriate that I start with one of the funniest stories about Sean. We had him and a bunch of people over at the house for a cookout. Sean, of course, was the life of the party, pretty normal. But suddenly he went missing for quite some time. I was wondering where he was when one of the girls at the party came up to me and said, 'Mike, I've been trying to use your bathroom for a while and the door's locked. I don't even know if anyone's in there.' Well, Sean had decided to take a shower in the middle of the party. I don't know why he did this because he had a shower at his apartment. Maybe he didn't have any soap or something, I don't know. But he was doing it because he cared about being clean and presentable to everybody there at the cookout. But Sean was so kind that he didn't want to use our towels—so he just put his clothes back on and drip-dried. You can do that in Colorado. (Thankfully we weren't in Ohio, because that doesn't work well there. You tend to get rashes when you do that in Ohio!)

"Anyway, the two of us would spend many nights at the Onyx, which was a gothic nightclub in the Capitol Hill area. It was the kind of place where they showed zombie and vampire movies on the TV screens in the bar—definitely not sports. I was the pastor who would tag along with Sean when he went there to dance, to relate, to share the gospel. (You have to understand that I am dressed in black today, not so much because it's a funeral but in honor of Sean. This is about as goth as I get!)

"I'd be at the Onyx dressed in black jeans and a black sweater out of respect for the culture. I'd feel out of place, even though Sean invited me, because I'm six foot three, well over 250 pounds, and very conspicuous. I would buy one beer for the evening just to try and hide behind it. (It's fascinating how you can go to a club and feel uncomfortable, but buy a beer, and merely by holding it, somehow you feel like you're blending in.) So, I would buy a beer, then he would go and dance and I would just sit there on the sidelines, sipping my beer. As I sat there, he would bring this constant parade of people up to me: 'This is my pastor, Mike Sares, from Scum of the Earth! You should talk to him!' I would consequently field all sorts of questions from predestination versus free will, to reincarnation versus resurrection, to seven-day creation to . . . It was one of those settings where I had to be on my toes every time. I went with Sean because these people had never talked to a pastor, much less a pastor at the Onyx.

"It was grand. It revolutionized my view of Capitol Hill. He was always pushing me, 'Mike, we have to do more at the Onyx! We should have a whole group of people here.' So a few times we had a group of folks come along with us: dancing, relating and sharing our faith in Christ. I never did get the courage to dance there, but I must admit that I have attempted it privately while in my home, trying to imitate Sean in front of my bedroom mirror. It's a sight.

"The thing about Sean is that he was an intentional missionary. You have to understand that he did not come from the goth culture, but he learned it. It was like the apostle Paul saying to the Jews, 'I become a Jew to the Jews, a Greek to the Greeks, and to those not under the law I become like one not under the law that

I may win all those people to Christ.' Make no mistake: Sean was a missionary to Capitol Hill, and he said so. He had a few supporters. He sent them letters. Sometimes I would read them over and wonder, 'How do you get anyone to support you with letters like this?' They weren't that well-written. But it was clear that he saw Capitol Hill as his mission field.

"A couple of very interesting conversations late in his life shed light on what was going on. To one young man he said, 'I think I need to get away from Capitol Hill. It's really dark. And it's starting to suck me in. I just need to get away. Maybe I'll go to Boulder and spread the gospel there.' To another person he said, 'I've done everything I know how to do in Capitol Hill. I have spread the gospel. I have passed out Bibles. I have brought people to church and to Bible studies. I think I need to go and find a different place to minister.' Even in his last desperate days, what was inside of him was this desire to share the love of Jesus with people.

"It's difficult to talk about Sean's passing because he didn't go the way we would have liked him to go. But he knew death was coming. I had an experience with Sean two years ago that I shared with his parents. I've shared it with very few people. We were having lunch at the Café Netherworld (also a goth hangout), and Sean was doing badly. He wasn't feeling very well. He had been struggling with his own personal demons and sat across the table from me a very haggard guy. He was sobering up from an alcoholic binge. We were eating lunch together when I heard this voice. It wasn't an audible voice, more like an impression on my heart. It was clear. I sensed it was God's voice because there was so much love in it for Sean, so much compassion. I was sitting there with him and it said, 'Sean is a fragile young man. And he is not going to be able to handle growing old. And so I am going to take him while he is still young.' The impression I received was that it would be soon.

"Now what do you do with that? You're a pastor. You've been to seminary. You've been in ministry for quite some time and you're going, *I* think *that was God. I have heard his voice before. Can I be sure? How do I respond?* So my reaction was to do everything I possibly could to keep that from happening for as long as possible. I wasn't trying to thwart God's will. I figured that he would do what he would do. In the meantime, I was to take care of Sean, and never tell him what I thought I heard.

"I rounded up some people from Scum of the Earth to come and to help out because I couldn't provide the kind of support that Sean needed all by myself. I knew that he had plenty of people around him, but in these last couple of years it's just been more and more difficult to help him. This was primarily because he was so darn stubborn. This did make him a great evangelist, however. And while it made him a great evangelist, it made him a really difficult parishioner. Our gifts are always a two-edged sword like that, aren't they? Strengths carry inherent weakness with them in this life. We began to help Sean through his stays in the Denver Cares detox center, hospital visits, emergency room visits, doctor's appointments, and halfway houses. Sometimes he would get really healthy for a while. Sometimes he would be back to the good old Sean and it was wonderful. But then he would slide back down.

"One time Sean and I were on our way back from one of the doctor's visits. A Christian pediatrician saw Sean for free but would always schedule him for the end of the day, when no little kids were there. He did this because Sean would walk into the office in full goth regalia, complete with eyeliner. The doctor didn't want the kids to get scared! On our way home from the doctor's office that day, Sean sat slumped in the passenger seat of my car. We were driving west on Colfax Avenue in the late afternoon. The sun was beginning its descent from the brilliant blue on high, sending huge beams of light through the breaks in the large, billowy clouds. The Rocky Mountains were firm and majestic on the horizon. It was a heavenly sight. Sean looked up at the sky, squinting a bit, and then said something that made my jaw hit the steering wheel. 'I'm going to die soon. God knows how much I want to be with him. He knows I don't like living here.' There it was, confirmation for a word from God that I had not wanted to hear.

"In 1 Corinthians 15:54-57, the apostle Paul talks about this whole dying process:

> Then, when our dying bodies have been transformed into bodies that will never die, this Scripture will be fulfilled. Death is swallowed up in victory. O death, where is your victory? O death, where is your sting? For sin is the sting that results in death, and the law gives sin its power. But thank God. He gives us victory over sin and death through our Lord Jesus Christ. (NLT)

"When Jesus was led to the cross and those nails went into his hands, the spear went into his side and he breathed his dying breath, I can imagine the hoards of the Evil One shouting in jubilation. They had killed the Messiah. But what they didn't know was what my friend Jim Emig says, that Satan's greatest victory is merely the foundation for God's greater victory. That is what Paul is talking about here. He is saying, 'You know what? Death is not the end. Death is not the death of our dreams. It's the doorway to the fulfillment of our most wonderful dreams.' The great saint is giving us a peek into eternity. He's saying, 'Look, Jesus loves you. Death's not the end. It's just the beginning.'

"I love thinking about a Sean who is no longer in torment. I love it. I don't know if any of us, except for the ones who struggle with the kind of liability where your mind won't work the way you want it to most of the time, can understand. I think the older Sean got, the less his mind worked the way he wanted it to; so he was often attempting to self-medicate to get the clarity that he wanted. Now, was he deceived into thinking that some of the things he was doing would bring him clarity? Yes, he was. You can say in some ways that Capitol Hill did him in, that the darkness overcame him. You could say that if you wanted to. But that's not the end of the story, because Satan's greatest victory is just the foundation for God's greater victory.

"Gothic Sean's death was not in vain. What I've seen today is evidence and testimony to that truth. So many people here have witnessed the saving love of Jesus Christ through this man. There are many more stories where those came from. Sean's last couple years in no way negate the force of his life lived in Christ—for even at the end he loved people in Jesus' name and was telling them about new life in Christ. If you have never considered submitting your life to Sean's Lord Jesus, by all means, today is the day. Maybe it's something you could do in his honor. Seriously consider the Lord Jesus that he spoke about so often. I've watched people on Capitol Hill dismiss Sean left and right as simply a Jesus freak, but those same people—when their lives were falling apart, guess who they came to talk to?

"I talked recently to one young woman who lived in Sean's apartment building. She told me that early one evening she was in bed and heard this knocking on her door. It was Sean. 'Come on out! Come out here! You gotta see this painting! It's huge! It's enormous! Come on out here!'

"She called to him from inside her apartment, 'Sean, I'm in bed! Leave me alone. I'm tired.'

"He kept right on. 'No! Open the door and look. It's stupendous!'

"'Well can't you just bring it in?' she asked.

"'It's too big to fit through the door!' Sean shouted. 'It won't fit in. You've got to come out here!' He was relentless, relentless like the Hound of Heaven, chasing you down, grabbing you by the leg and bringing you to Jesus. He was so insistent that she finally got up, put on her robe and came out. Sean said, 'Look!' And what she saw was a sunset beyond anything you could have brought into that small apartment.

"I think what Sean is saying to all of us is: 'It's huge, it's tremendous. You have no idea of the wonders that God has for those who love him. More than any eye can see, more than any mind can imagine are the joys waiting for those who call on the name of Jesus, because no one gets out of here alive.' There is a door to this life, and when it swings wide open, we will encounter the risen Jesus on the other side in all of his glory.

"I trust that Jesus is in heaven praying for us as our High Priest, according to what the Scripture says. And I think that Sean is in heaven praying for us as his assistant. I really do. I mean, aren't we supposed to be like Jesus? What would Jesus do on earth? Isn't that what we are to do while we are here? Well, what does Jesus do in heaven? He prays, for one thing, and I wouldn't be surprised if that's what we are to do there with him. But for now, I'm going to pray this old Orthodox prayer, hundreds and hundreds of years old, for my friend Gothic Sean. Will you please join me?

Oh God of Spirits and of all flesh, you have trampled down death and abolished the power of the devil giving life to your world. Thank you for giving rest to the soul of your departed servant Sean in a place of light, in a place of repose, in a place of refreshment where there is no pain, sorrow and suffering. As a good and loving Savior, thank you for forgiving every sin he committed in thought, word or deed; for there is no one who lives and is sinless. You alone are without sin. Your righteousness is an everlasting righteousness, and your word is truth. For you, Christ our God, are the resurrection, the life and the repose of your departed servant Sean. To you we give glory with your eternal Father and your all-holy, good and life-giving Spirit, now and forever, to the ages of ages.

May your memory be eternal dear brother; for you are worthy of blessedness and everlasting memory in Christ Jesus. Amen.

9

Art

Dancing in the Pen

We work hard with our own hands.

I'm married to an artist. I remember when Mary and I were dating, I would stop by her parents' house during the summer when she was home from graduate school. She would be hunched over, working on some project. I'm somewhat of an artist myself, though not the visual kind. I like to write stories and lyrics and sometimes a little bit of music. So we produced children who are artists as well. Our oldest daughter is a visual artist with a master's degree in the fine arts. Our second daughter is an actress and a good singer. Our two sons have both become better guitar players than their father and are visual artists to boot.

The artistic temperament is a difficult one to deal with, not just at home but in the church. The things that make artists sensitive to beauty and truth are the same things that can make it difficult for them to get along with others. Let's face it: artists are not accountants. Many of them cannot handle their finances, much less their emotions. There's an old joke among pastors that when Satan fell from heaven, he fell into the worship team. (I think that joke says more about the inability of senior pastors to get along with artists than it does about theology!) Of course there are exceptions, but the tortured, angst-filled, manic-depressive artist is a typical character that everyone recognizes in books, in film or in their personal lives.

I love artists. I love the passion they bring to life and to the church. I think that artists are at times prophetic in their gifting, telling us truths that even the best preachers can only hint at.

Consider, for example, the truth that can be found in architecture. The Gothic cathedral is itself a metaphor. From the outside, a Gothic church building such as Notre Dame in Paris looks massive, foreboding and even a little bit scary. The windows are dark, the exterior is colorless. There are gargoyles—demonic-looking creatures—adorning the downspouts all over the outside of the cathedral and spewing water when it rains. The person on the outside has no inkling what he or she is missing on the inside, both literally and metaphorically. But once inside the church, the worshiper is bathed in light—and not just any old light. Thousands of pieces of stained glass throw light of every imaginable hue all over the cathedral and the worshiper. There is art in the ornate altars and the carvings in stone and wood. Statues and paintings of great people who have gone before are all around. And of course, inside the cathedral we find Christ—depictions of his life, death and resurrection. Thus, the Gothic cathedral becomes a metaphor for one's journey from the outer darkness to the light of God's kingdom. It is a metaphor of our conversion.

A tour of the history of Western art shows its incredible Christian roots. As the church gained legitimacy, money and power, it began spending money on the arts. Even during the Protestant

Reformation, artists continued to paint, to write music, to sculpt and to write literature in the light of the truth of the gospel.

What makes Christian art? Is Christian art whatever art is created by a Christian, or is Christian art about a certain subject matter? Can a painting of a homeless man be just as "Christian" as a painting of the Last Supper?

One musician friend of mine says that "some people sing about the light, while others sing about what they see because of the light." I believe that we too often relegate Christian music to songs "about the light." Christian radio hits are almost exclusively songs about God or sung to God, as opposed to being about anything else we deal with on a daily basis.

Most people at Scum don't listen to Christian music. I was surprised by this, to be honest. I grew up as a part of the Jesus movement. For us, contemporary Christian music was a breath of fresh air. Listening to Randy Stonehill, Phil Keaggy and others sing about life from a Christian perspective was a new experience. The only other rock musicians we knew of were singing about drugs, sex or some Eastern religion.

Over the years contemporary Christian music shifted to singing almost exclusively about the light and not about the things that were seen as a result of the light. Add a lot of money to the mix, and this new Christian music became an industry that kept putting out more of the same. Bring this thirty years forward, and Christian bands lack street credibility with the kinds of people who come to Scum.

Musicians in the contemporary Christian music industry primarily play churches and Christian music festivals. But in its heyday Reese's band, Five Iron Frenzy, would intentionally book shows in bars and clubs around their church appearances. It was the only way they could keep getting the word out about Jesus to those that yearned for some good news. The band needed the

Christian shows to survive financially. Those gigs are more prof-
itable than playing bars and nightclubs, to be honest. But they
needed the secular shows to survive spiritually.

Sounds backward, doesn't it? Maybe that's one reason they
never won a Dove award.

Being pastor to Five Iron Frenzy was an education for me.
Here was a group of passionate, committed Christians who
wanted to make a difference in the world and attempted to walk
the narrow line between what it meant to be a Christian band and
what it meant to be a regular band. They wrote songs, like "Sucker
Punch," about teenage angst. They wrote songs about falling in
love and breaking up, a story common to everybody whether
Christian or non-Christian. On the other hand, they wrote songs
like "Every New Day" that are unabashed hymns to God. They
were invited on several tours with non-Christian bands and still
played all the main Christian festivals. They enjoyed performing,
traveling and being "rock stars," but they also formed a Bible
study, helped start a church, helped to build an orphanage in
Mexico and were committed to helping other bands whenever
they could—even if it meant becoming temporary roadies.

Hundreds of thousands of young men and women heard Five
Iron Frenzy play over the years (and still do, thanks to CDs and
the Internet). They came to Jesus or were nurtured in their faith
by the band's music and lyrics. The lyrics were sermons; the
music was worship at its most energetic. There is no way, of
course, that membership in any band's fan club can match the
life-changing dynamic of being in a local church. Thank God
the band knew that. But that being said, I think of Five Iron
Frenzy as having been something like pastors of a multinational
ska-core church.

One of the reasons for Five Iron Frenzy's success and longevity
was the band's commitment to be under some kind of spiritual

authority. And so they brought their artistic energy and sensibilities to Scum of the Earth.

They weren't immune to relational difficulties. One time two of them got in a fistfight, in front of fans after a concert. And four years into his time with the band, their guitar player, Scott Kerr, a brilliant young man raised in a Christian home, found himself going through a crisis of faith. Did he still believe all the things he had been taught since he was a child? Was it his parents' faith or his own? What about all the questions that had never been adequately answered in his mind about the sovereignty of God and suffering? Scott had too much integrity to keep playing the songs he had written while having these profound doubts, so he left to study and figure things out.

The rest of the band members were left in a shambles. How could this happen to one of their own? Could they have done anything to prevent his leaving? Scott was one of the leaders of the band, and he was questioning God; where did that leave the rest of them and their unanswered questions?

I took Five Iron Frenzy on a prayer retreat right after they chose Sonnie Johnson as Scott's replacement. The band was excited about its future with its new member but still grieving the loss of one of its founders. The prayer retreat ended up being one of the most significant periods of time we ever had. The presence of God was palpable. Years later, Dennis Culp wrote about it in the song "It Was Beautiful."

We flew over Alaska;
we saw the frozen mountains pierce the clouds.
It was beautiful.

We felt the waves of New Zealand;
the water shimmered beneath a moonlight shroud.
It was beautiful.

Close to home in an ordinary room
We felt You there. It's my favorite memory.
You're so beautiful.

The spring in Appalachia,
with flowers swaying above the fields of green.
It was beautiful.

Driving in New England,
the road littered with bright October leaves.
It was beautiful.

Close to home in an ordinary room
We felt You there. It's my favorite memory.
You're so beautiful to me.

Thanks for the songs, these seven friends and eight good
        years.
It is You that made them sweet.
It was beautiful.

Pictures looking back,
just snapshots of the past cannot compare,
to feeling what we felt, through anything that came,
that You were there.

A thousand smiling faces,
backlit and bouncing to the beat.
It was beautiful.

As many soaring voices,
forever changed by Your mercy.
It was beautiful.

Far away from all the lights and noise we felt You there.
It's my favorite memory.

You're so beautiful to me.

Thanks for the songs, these seven friends and eight good
years.
It is You that made them sweet.
You're so beautiful to me.

The final retreat for Five Iron Frenzy was at a Young Life
camp near Fraser, Colorado, where the band decided to call it
quits. They had weathered seven years of financial, emotional
and interpersonal ups and downs. They would have kept going
in spite of all of that, but now they were older. Many of them
were married, some couples were thinking about having children. Their frustration over not being able to reach an audience
that was predominantly non-Christian (what bands like Relient
K and Switchfoot were eventually able to accomplish) were taking their toll. Slowly but surely as we prayed and talked, it became obvious that God was closing the book on Five Iron
Frenzy. They had begun and continued the band's career by
sensing his pleasure. Now it seemed God's pleasure was for them
to end well.

I can't stress enough how unusual it is for most bands, even
most Christian bands, to end well. Normally the things that break
up bands are an inability to get along with one another, egos that
spin out of control, fights with record labels and the like. But here
was a band that determined before the Lord to end as they had
begun, holding each others' hands and staying friends through
their last concert together. So Five Iron Frenzy planned its demise
fifteen months before it actually occurred.

Rumors of the band's breakup had been flying around the Internet for years. In response, the band had promised that they
would give their fans a year's notice. So in September 2002, Five
Iron Frenzy planned for its last show in November 2003. They

called their final tour "Winners Never Quit," once again poking fun at themselves and maintaining a humble attitude that would honor Christ. They knew that Jesus is for quitters.

I see my job as a pastor being to prepare the saints for works of service so that the body of Christ may be built up (Eph 4:12). When it came to Five Iron Frenzy, I felt that I did my job, and it brought me great joy. In order for the relationship of artists and the church to survive, special care and time has to be devoted to it. Yet often artists are given little attention by pastors. When a pastor does spend time with the artists in the church, however, the blessings to both can be massive, and the church at large is strengthened. It may not be without controversy, however.

THE POETRY INCIDENT

A few days before Christmas 2001, I got a call from Reese. "Mary Kate Makkai has agreed to read one of her poems at the Christmas Eve service. It's really, really good, but it's got the F-bomb in it several times, and I just thought I should check with you about that." We always have several original poems read as part of our Christmas Eve liturgy, so Reese's request was not surprising. The F-bomb, however, caught me off guard.

I told Reese that I couldn't give him an answer yet. I trusted Reese when it came to lyrics and such, so my first inclination was to say, "Go ahead," but I just wasn't sure. I had known Mary Kate (who usually just went by "Kate") for years. I had met her when she was a student at a local Christian college. Even back then I could tell that she was struggling with her faith. The confines of Christian subculture were suffocating her individuality and artistic spirit. We hit it off right away. She was the roommate of the only girl in Five Iron Frenzy, Leanor Ortega, and the two of them made a dynamic duo. Scum of the Earth hadn't even been conceived, but I soon became her pastor. She would talk with my wife and me for hours. Kate would even show up at our family's Greek Easter dinners!

After Kate finished college we kept in contact, but she left the Christian subculture almost completely. In a lot of ways, she was like the young son in Luke 15. She went down a long prodigal journey with her faith. During that time she had become a part of the slam poetry community. The girl was good—better than her teachers. She started winning slam poetry competitions around the country. And then, at long last, she found herself returning to her faith. She had not been present at the founding of Scum, but almost two years later she was taking a tentative step inside.

One of the things that led Kate back was her work in poetry therapy with juvenile delinquents. In these angry young boys she saw a reflection of herself, and she recognized that her love for them was not unlike God's love for her. The poem that she had written for our Christmas Eve service, a chronicle of her own journey back to God, quoted some of the boys' foul language. Therein lay the problem.

I wanted to give Kate a place to use her gift at Scum of the Earth. I felt that asking Kate to clean the poem up before presenting it in church would be like asking the widow to wipe off her coins before dropping them in the offering plate. I also sensed it would be as important for us to hear the poem as for her to deliver it, but I needed to check with some trusted advisors before I could make the decision. I called two pastors who were friends of mine, a seminary professor and—since pastors at Scum fundraise their salary—some of my financial supporters.

The two supporters—good people whose combined time in the faith had been at least seventy years—were dead set against allowing the F-word to be used in the context of a worship service. The pastors, however, were a bit more gray about it. They saw that Kate was at a critical stage in her journey back to God, and they advised me to be careful not to squelch her.

Beyond the pastoral implications, I also explored the theological and biblical issues with Craig Blomberg from Denver Seminary. He noted that while the Bible is obviously a wonderful book, if you take some parts out of the broader context, you're going to find rape, incest, sodomy, murder—all sorts of terrible things. Context became central to my decision.

Mary Kate's poem was about someone coming back to the Lord, which is a wonderful context. In the middle of that context, she quotes someone else who is very angry at life and uses poor language. Dr. Blomberg and I went on to discuss Ephesians 5, which talks about foolish talk and coarse joking. We didn't feel the poem fell under either category; the poem was not a crude attempt at humor, and it was not immoral.

After that, I had to think of what might be considered obscene in my own congregation. For many of the people who come to Scum, the F-bomb is just another means of expressing frustration. However, if Kate were to stand in front of the congregation (or anyone, for that matter) and hurl the F-bomb during an argument, it would not be OK. We are never to speak to one another in that manner. Scripture is clear about that. But that wasn't what she was doing. She wasn't taking God's name in vain or asking God to damn someone to hell. She was quoting an angry adolescent boy in the story of her own trek back to Jesus. This poem was being spoken as an honest hymn of redemption.

I was satisfied that there existed no scriptural prohibition against reading the poem in church, but I also had to consider the inevitable fallout that "to bomb or not to bomb" would produce. I knew it was going to insult some people, and might really hurt my relationships with some of my supporters. And yet if I did not allow Kate to read the poem, it would be yet another time the sensibilities of Christians had exasperated her attempts at authenticity. I had to decide whom I was going to offend—the young woman who was tentatively placing her foot into the door of the church for the first time in years, or mature, faithful Christians who might leave me and Scum of the Earth but never leave Jesus and his church.

You know which option I went with, I'll bet. If you can't attempt this kind of thing at Scum, where in the body of Christ are you gonna do it? (Not even, apparently, in a book about Scum.)

To her credit, Mary Kate cut the F-bombs in half for the evening. It probably didn't lessen the impact very much. I issued a warning that this part of the service was going to be rated R, and then she began to read her poem, "Lost & Found."

Here,
in this latest heart-broken ocean,
I'm gathering tears like tired, salt sea-shells
from the rock bottom beach of my face

but it's
too deep
too much
too hard
too now
to tolerate the next ten seconds to ten seconds later
hoping later will find this tolerable.
My pastor, friend with me fidgets, shrugs, asks:
"Kate, where are you with God?"

Now
Picture
Boy, 15, poetry class
his barely man-tinted face
eyes pressed to an empty page that confronts him

like his father's fist.
He pen-pecks his frustration,
scribbled false starts crowding line upon line.
He looks around a roomful of other delinquents,
all writing,
slowly untangling new-born thoughts that could gut you
with fresh-sharpened truth.

Boy scowls,
scrawls a deep savage ZAG in place of the
curses he can't spell
pain he can't identify
desires he can't articulate
and announces that he can't do this
doesn't want to . . .

I wish I could capture the emotion in Kate's voice that night.
Listening to her insightful and passionate retelling of this epi-
sode from her soul's migration was astonishing. I was the "pastor, friend" she had spoken of, yet even I had only an inkling of
the intense battle she'd been in to express the pain within her
heart to God.

At this point in the poem, the kid launched a tirade of abuse
against everyone in his life, including his poetry-therapy facilita-
tor. And so, of course, this was also the place in her poem that
Kate began quoting her student's use of the dreaded expletive.
Most of the young adults at Scum had heard that kind of language
every day at work, on campus or in the streets. They knew that
the kid in the poem was really, really angry. But he was a pathetic
figure as well. "Listen to him," Kate pleaded with us,

    his child-shaped ghost rattling chain to chain to chain-link
        fence

throwing barb-wire shadows against his last chance
and the too many years left to live like this . . .

I looked from Kate to the crowd. There were people crammed everywhere. The ones up in the balcony were sitting with their faces pressed to the banister, their legs hanging loosely between the rails. On the main level, they sat on the floor leaning forward with legs folded or hugging their knees—motionless. In my memory, no one was even blinking. Here, on a Christmas Eve, we were watching what appeared to be Kate's "last chance." She didn't want to live like this anymore. She had, unlike the boy in her poem, scrawled a fascinating, aesthetic ZAG deeper than he'd ever imagined. It was mesmerizing.

Kate's student emerged after two hours of throwing obscenities to stand in front of her with a single piece of paper. Mary Kate Makkai stood before Scum of the Earth Church, "that same dangling, ripped-raged boy, standing paper in hand . . ." after many more hours wrestling with the Almighty. She had experienced a blessed surrender, not unlike the pupil of whom she wrote.

In the poem, the raging storm had waned. The boy finally read his poem aloud:

I . . . am . . . not a . . . bad person.

One line as stark as an unshaded lightbulb
in an empty white room . . .
and hung against all this technicolor poetry spangle.

But hear
the prayer sparked embers
of this boy
lifting this torch
into the midnight of his own apathy

as he wrings his first declarative statement from his third-
    grade vocabulary
Here
God is ink-blue, song-stained, dancing in the pen,
in the hand of the boy who is beginning to understand
the soul difference between good and bad
is what you learned from it.

And I have seen boys
scorched ashen with despair,
writhe loose, slide into quiet imagination
and compose love letters to the color blue.
Marching their merciless journey to a statistical manhood
bound   beaten   worthless   hopeless
each word stamped like a boot into the face of their futures
boy answers:
I   am   not
and writes it down to remind himself.

My boys
you remind me
to get up
get on with it
you remind me that flowers can bloom through stone
remind me that Jesus Christ promised heaven to a dying
    thief
remind me that it has to get darker before you can see the
    stars
you
even here in this latest heart-broken ocean
this is where I am with God

with you.

When Kate finished her dramatic reading, there was a stunned silence throughout the large room. I wasn't sure if people were in shock or awe. It lasted about three seconds. Then, spontaneously, there came thunderous applause and cheering. It was the most dynamic moment I have experienced in a worship service. Some people were weeping. It was incredible.

After the service, I received e-mails from a number of young adults in the congregation:

Mike, I just wanted to express my appreciation for the risk you took. My sister, she's 17. We grew up in the church. But she has been drifting really far, doesn't consider herself a Christian anymore. And she came.

We were driving home. She said that the poem really touched her. She talked about how it was so real. So raw. The emotion. How it is so true that to see stars, the sky has to get dark. She was really touched and encouraged by the poem.

So. I just wanted to give you encouragement. Let you know that I agree with the decision. I am praying for you. Take care.

–Tim

Hi, Mike. Merry Christmas. I know this is kind of random, but I wanted to tell you what I thought about last night's Christmas Eve Service. That service was one of the most powerful Christmas services I've ever attended, and I have been brought up in the church.

In her poem was a picture of how God meets me. How he speaks to my heart. It was one of the most poignant pictures of modern day redemption I have heard. It moved me to tears. And I watched the faces of my friends, whose hearts have been jaded by the hypocrisy in the church; and they softened. I hung out with dozens of kids after Scum that night. And all they spoke of was the poem. How it was real. How it was raw.

It was a shock that church was real. Which meant God was real. And if God wasn't shocked by the language they used everyday, maybe, just maybe, they could talk to Him.

So I just wanted to thank you, Mike. Because it took a lot of courage to allow that in your service. I wanted to say thanks—from all of us that left there shocked—shocked that God was that real, and we could be that real with Him. And all of us who said, "Now that is why this is my church." Thank you.

–Skyler

Not everyone responded approvingly. There were a few who left to go outside before the poem began. At least one person was upset because those people felt compelled to leave, and there were a few who didn't like what they heard. Relationships were torn that night with some of my staunchest supporters.

I am sad to this day that I could not please both sides in this dilemma. I understand a bit of what those dear folks were defending. I think they were choosing for the holiness of God and reverence, especially on Christmas Eve. They would say that we should bring our best before God, including our best use of language. I am grateful for Scum's friends who disagreed with the decision to allow "Lost & Found" to be read that night. They remind me that God is worthy of respect and honor. They remind me that I am but dust and a recipient of fantastic mercy. I look forward to spending eternity with them in a perfect place inhabited by perfected saints.

I worked hard over the next several months to repair those relationships as best I could. I am happy to say that we are friends to this day. One of the guys even helped me paint my house! Mary Kate continues to follow Jesus and stay in relationship with those in the church. She has read her poetry at more than a few services since. (None of them contained the F-bomb. Not that it matters . . .)

I can't imagine Scum of the Earth without artists. I can't imagine any church without artists. I can't imagine the history or the future of the church without artists. We'd be the poorer for it, that's for sure. Artists are essential to God's will for the body of Christ. Working out any problems they may cause for the rest of us is what we're meant to do, for the good of us all.

10

Love

God's Policy

When we are cursed, we bless.

I was an English education major in college. I remember one of my professors saying something *sorta kinda* to the effect of "fuzzy language produces fuzzy thinking." When our language is vague, so is our understanding.

The most vague word in the English language may be *love.* Christians throw the word around a lot. We're supposed to love God and love others. We're supposed to love our families and even our enemies. But we also love espresso in the morning. We love pizza at night. We just love those new shoes. And instead of saying goodbye when we hang up the phone, we say to our acquaintances, "Love ya!"

Coming from a Greek background, I always knew that there were more words that Greeks would use to describe what Americans call love. For the ancient Greeks, family love is characterized in the word *storge*. It is bred from familiarity. We don't choose our parents, and while parents may beget children they certainly don't get to choose DNA structure, personality types or even gender. As such, anyone can be loved by *storge*— the ugly, the stupid, the exasperating. Even different species can love each other with *storge*. Pet owners experience this kind of affection for their dogs and cats. Even the dog and the cat themselves might show this kind of affection toward each other. One of the reasons my wife puts up with me is because being with a man whose idiosyncrasies she knows is better than being with a man of unknown "grossities." That's the same reason, I think, that most parents would never trade their teens with another family's teens. At least they know what to expect from their own.

Storge, affectionate love, thus becomes a base for the other loves. It leads us to endure and then to enjoy those with whom otherwise we wouldn't associate. We can find real goodness in a place that under other circumstances we would never choose to look. We handpick our friends, but *storge* allows us to develop a deep affection for people we are required to be with, such as neighbors, coworkers and roommates.

Storge is not, however, totally altruistic. This is best illustrated, says C. S. Lewis, by the picture of a mother nursing her baby. Sure, she is sustaining that tiny person's existence, but there is also something in it for her. If she skips a couple feedings, mom is crying as well as the baby. *Storge* is a love that we *need* to give, as well as to receive.

By giving *storge* we expect something in return—familiarity, comfort, the same old routine. Woe to the child who takes an interest in something the family has never appreciated, whether it be classical music or macramé. Woe to the grown-up younger brothers who wish to change the routine of big sister's care for them, a situation of *storge*-gone-bad about which C. S. Lewis actually wrote an epitaph in his *Poems*.

> Erected by her sorrowing brothers
> In memory of Martha Clay.
> Here lies one who lived for others.
> Now she has peace, and so have they.

Once *storge* goes bad, it becomes stifling. A loving mother becomes a smother-mother. Protective fathers become control freaks. Ladies in the church become . . . well, church-ladies. *Storge*-gone-bad is what happened between me and some of the women of the Greek Orthodox Church about a year or so after my conversion experience. I was in college and on fire with my newfound faith in Christ, so I volunteered to teach the senior-high Sunday school class. We talked about how radical Jesus was in the Gospel stories. I'd bring my guitar and lead the students in songs that I had learned from my Young Life buddies.

This was anything but the same old routine. This was not what some of the women expected to take place in our very traditional Orthodox Church. This was not the familiar curriculum they wanted for their children. They talked to the priest. He talked to me. "You're causing division in the church, Michael," he said. "So you're going to have to stop teaching the senior high Sunday school class." These otherwise wonderful folks had watched me grow up. They were friends of my family, but I had crossed the line of what they were accustomed to.

Storge-gone-bad is also why people who consider themselves family sometimes talk to each other and act toward each other in ways they would never talk or act with outsiders. Since home is a place where manners may not be required, we can mistakenly assume that they are not needed. I can recall, to my own shame, arguments in the car with Mary or my children on the way to church. As soon as the car entered the church parking lot, my demeanor would change and the volume of my voice would drop. I was getting ready to be a Christian, after all. The church family I was about to enter was not as familiar as my own family. While real *storge*-love is a beautiful thing, it also has its downside.

That's *storge*. The other kinds of love I grew up learning about—*philia* and *eros*—are located outside the family. Consequently, they invite some degree of confusion. The young adults at Scum of the Earth ask me these kinds of questions on a regular basis:

"Can I just be friends with a girl I'm romantically attracted to?"

"Can I just be friends with the boy I recently broke up with?"

"Can men and women be friends at all without romance happening?"

I think that men and women can be friends as long as the typical rules of friendship are present. I also think that if a man and woman are friends, there's a better-than-average chance that friendship will morph into romance within the first half hour—at least for one of them.

By *eros* the Greeks were talking about romance, the state of "being in love." *Eros* is expressed in the hours spent just thinking about the person with whom one is in love. *Eros* isn't lust; sexual desire wants only to feel pleasure, whereas *eros* wants the whole person. I don't think that my marriage depends on *eros* much of the time, but it is what got me into marriage. Like nuclear fusion, it can be constructive or destructive. Under the influence of *eros*, a young man might plan a romantic evening out on the town with his wife and then seduce her at home, or he might run off with her best friend after a concert.

The emotions of romance can be likened to skydiving. You're in the plane. Your chute is securely fastened. Your heart is pounding and you are scared out of your mind. Finally, with great effort, you use your arms and legs to push yourself out of the plane's open door. The feeling is exhilarating. You're floating and everything is beautiful. But once you hit the ground, it's life as normal. You've got to get up, pack up your parachute, and start walking. (This presumes, of course, that you had the good sense to pull your rip cord on the way down.)

Philia, or friendship, is by contrast about similar ideals, shared goals and like passions. Lewis compares *philia* to romantic love in *The Four Loves:* "Lovers are always talking to one another about their love; friends hardly ever about their friendship. Lovers are usually face to face, absorbed in each other, friends, side by side absorbed in some common interest."

I commonly hear a young person from Scum saying about his beloved, "She is my best friend." At that point, I begin asking questions. "Does she enjoy video games as much as you do?" "Is she a Star Wars geek like you are?" "Is she into fixed gear bicycling as much as you are?" "Do you read the same books?" "Are you into knitting like she is?" "Do you enjoy long British romance novels that have been made into movies like she does?" "When she asks you to go out dancing, do you make up some excuse about staying home to water your cactus?"

Lewis would say that if lovers were friends, they would be just as concerned about each other's naked personalities as their naked bodies. In addition to the romance, they'd love to talk, hear each other's opinion on topics that they both hold dear, learn how each other would react in situations in which they find themselves, and so on. Any friendship that Mary and I have is not based on *eros* but on *philia*—a similar sense of humor, our love of the theater, the fact that we were both English majors in college, the fact that we both come from immigrant families, and the fact that we both like God (a lot). Would we still be friends if the blazing fires of *eros* turned into glowing embers? Would we still be able to relate to each other when romantic feelings for each other have fled away?

If the answer is yes, then we are friends.

Friendship, by its very nature, implies a degree of exclusivity. To say "You are my friend" is also to say that others are not. Friendship provides insulation and comfort from the outside world. But friendship itself should be critiqued from the outside. Friends can enhance one another's vices as well as their virtues. Like *eros, philia* isn't the kind of love that can police itself. Since friends tend to think alike, they rarely hear contradicting opinions that help them be wise in their decisions. People have got themselves into all kinds of trouble by just listening to their friends.

Similarly, *eros* speaks in a big voice. Its passion is godlike. It is totally idealistic. While under the influence of romantic love, people make huge promises without being asked. "I will love you forever," we claim. "I will lasso the moon for you," we promise. This is where *eros* gets people into trouble. How many times have we seen the following scene in a movie? A girlfriend has just finished fixing her boyfriend a lovely meal on the rooftop of her apartment building. There are candles. There are wine glasses upon a white linen tablecloth. But he's been delayed. He can't make it. Soon the food is going cold and so is her heart; she starts drinking the wine all by herself. She had planned for *eros* to arrive, but it got stuck in traffic.

Like a garden, *eros* is incapable of maintaining itself. The promises we have made while under its influence are not necessarily kept. The feelings that caused us to make those promises don't last. *Eros* is capricious. We can't control its arrival or departure, we can only enjoy it when it shows up. *Eros*-gone-bad becomes something like a garden too near an atomic blast, yielding a giant, radioactive, killer tomato that starts absorbing everything in its path. Spoiled *eros* is obsessive and controlling. It becomes jealous, possessive, exacting and resentful. It's what stalkers are made of. If we have not experienced corrupted *eros,* then we have seen it in someone else. It can be very scary. What is a person in love to do?

Enter the hero, *agape,* the savior of all the other loves! While *agape* is a Greek word, modern Greeks don't use it the way it was defined a couple of millennia ago. Indeed, it seems foreign to just about everyone. In the other loves we get something in return for our investment. *Agape* gives and gives again without expecting in return. It loves in the face of pain. It cares for the unlovable without getting paid back in time, money or affection. *Agape* takes risks.

To be the object of *agape* is difficult. We've done nothing to earn it, and that is a shock. Please, love me for what I can do for you—my cleverness, usefulness, generosity—but don't love me with *agape!* What would that do to my self-image? Songwriter Sam Phillips captures that idea in her song "Don't Do Anything."

I, I love you
When you don't, when you don't do anything
When you're useless
I love you more
When you don't do anything
When you don't move, when you don't try
When you don't say anything
When you don't move, when you don't win
When you don't make anything look
I, I love you
When you don't
When you don't do anything
When you don't want, when you don't lie
When you don't make any sense
When you don't go, when you don't hide

When you don't think anything
I, I love you
When you don't
When you don't do anything
When you're useless
I love you more
When you don't do anything

When my wife loves me this way, I am flustered. I question her motives—what does she want? She couldn't be loving me for no reason, could she? The problem is that I no longer have control. She is operating beyond my reach. She doesn't even make a big deal about it (which proves, by the way, that it is *agape*). Real *agape*-love works best in secret. The object of its affections doesn't even realize when she or he is being loved in this manner. It is not enough for a husband to spend time with his young wife merely to assure her that she is loved. Sometimes that's the best the young man can do. He is on the road toward loving his wife; however, if spending time with her was the thing that he wanted to do above all others at that time—that would be *agape*.

I bring up this concept of love a lot at Scum, especially during weddings like Joshua and Liann's, two staff members at Scum. As of this writing, these newlyweds are traversing these United States in a converted veggie-oil-burning short bus as itinerant ministers under the umbrella of Scum of the Earth Church. Their bicycles are stored inside the bus along with an herb garden, baskets of fruit and veggies, and a bed.

Joshua and Liann met because a mutual friend thought they reminded her of each other, so she introduced them—through Myspace.com! I remember how enthusiastic Joshua was when he saw her pictures. They continued their relationship by writing to each other almost daily over Facebook, having long talks over the phone, and flying back and forth to visit one another in their respective cities. (That would be *eros*.) Lo and behold, their mutual friend was right. They did have a lot in common—love of metal music, bicycling, recycling, homiletics and Jesus. (That would be *philia*.) Liann moved from Chicago to Denver and immediately became part of the Scum community. Their wedding was of, by and for the church community and their families. Everything was homemade, from the decorations to the food to the music to the pedi-cab ride after the service. (That would be *storge*.)

Joshua and Liann's relationship had plenty of *storge, philia* and *eros* almost from the moment it began. For my message at their wedding, I wanted to concentrate on *agape*. I titled my message that day "When Love Is Policy."

"Joshua and Liann," I told them, "today is the day you begin to really love each other. You may have thought that you've been loving each other all along, but now it's different. Now you'll be committed. In some sense, you will *have* to love each other now, just because you're married. Before, there was no formal vow. Before, you had the option to go away. Now you have to stay. Before, love was a feeling. Now it's policy.

"You may think that I'm taking a dour look at marriage. I'm actually taking a very lofty view. You're about to promise to love each other for the rest of your lives. That mirrors the kind of promise God gives to every one of us. He loves us when it's not romantic. He loves us when we ignore him and don't talk with him. He loves us when we do things our own way, with no thought of what he would want. He loves us when we're bad— and I don't mean naughty; I mean really, really bad. The Bible even leads us to believe that he loves us all the more as we run away from him. That is love committed to us beyond feelings. It's God's policy to love us.

"I would like it to be your policy toward each other. I would like you to love each other when it's not romantic. Love when the other one of you is bad—and I don't mean naughty; I mean really, really bad. Love each other even after you've just got done cursing each other, whether silently or out loud. And if you sense the other one running away in some manner—emotionally or physically—love all the more, the way God loves you with patience, kindness, without envy, without boasting, without pride, without being rude, without being self-seeking, without anger, keeping no record of wrongs, not delighting in evil but rejoicing with the truth, always protecting, always trusting, always hoping, always persevering, never failing.

"Even though loving each other this way is what you *should* do, you won't. You can't. It's impossible. You'll spend a lifetime trying and failing. Let's face it, only God can love you that way. He doesn't love you just because He *has* to. It wouldn't be real love if he did it out of mere obligation. It's the thing he desires most: to love you. Loving you is his policy, but he's passionate about that policy."

If you want to learn woodworking, you go to a carpenter. If you want to learn metal forging, you go to a steel worker. If you want to learn loving, you go to God, for God is love. You can drive a steel spike through his hands into a piece of solid wood, and he will keep on loving you. We're called to follow God in this passionate policy, to learn from his example, to love one another because we each have been loved by God himself.

Agape is a gift from God. It could be no other. We will spend an eternity trying to understand it, for this is the way that we are loved by God. The church has no idea how much it is loved by Jesus. *I* have no idea how much I am loved by Jesus. If I did, I wouldn't so cavalierly break his heart while making my life miserable. If the church did, it might have a better reputation.

The apostle John wrote that "there is no fear in love. But perfect love drives out fear, because fear has to do with punishment.

The one who fears is not made perfect in love" (1 John 4:18). How many of us live fearing God's punishment on a regular basis? We still believe that Christianity is about following the rules, but it is not. God wants our lives to be shaped by the wonders of his mercy and his grace. He wants us to spend our lives trying to grasp that he doesn't give us the punishment we deserve but instead gives us love that we don't deserve. If we understood how completely we are loved in Christ, our gratitude would birth in us the kind of thoughts, words and deeds that are free from the threat of punishment anyway—for that is how it will all end up.

The older I get in Christ, the more I see this as the key to living a beautiful, holy life, pleasing to God. How else could I respond to a Creator who loves me when I don't do anything—and loves me even more when I run away? Mary Kate Makkai has a poem about *agape*. "Psalm" speaks about the faithfulness of a pursuing Christ who loves us at our worst, beckoning the best possible response.

Sometimes you can feel your heart slam shut
Like a hand covering a mouth that's just spoken 10,000 curses against a life that flows with all the grace and continuity of sideways snagging chunks of sour sadness wedged in the grinding mouth of time . . .

Sometimes you can feel your heart slam shut like a door to an empty room closes, locking 4 painfully bare walls in with each other . . . and you ache like a bright white under a harsh light that can't forgive what it's shining on

Sometimes you can feel your heart slam shut, and it withers like a stretch of unguarded skin beneath the burning sun-scorched weight of resentment, anger, fear, and hate feels like a block of ice laying heavy on your chest . . . your chest nothing but a threadbare sheet wearing silhouettes of your mistakes as it plays these tangy tragedies against your soul until you feel like nothing more than a wound too large to bandage

Every word you speak flails like a hand outstretched, reaching for anyone, anything to pull you out of this desperate dangling, almost falling, still clinging in spite of the nothing you'd like to hurl yourself into, because even that nothing must feel better than this, and that better must be somewhere nearby because it seems no one else is having this much trouble finding it, but you're blind, groping for something you've lost that's moved out of the radius of your grasp.

It's times like this,
When I feel like a solo harmonica, lost and wandering the shadowy caverns of human emotion, and I spend days knitting myself ragged gray scarves from the invisible threads that anchor me to this world . . . What can I say?

This is where he finds me . . .
this is the song I sing when all others have drained from my lips, and sorrow is the only color in my eyes, this is where he finds me . . . where I have no breath left for weeping and I'm wedged into the darkened corners, hiding in closets, under the tyranny of my own pounding fists.

This is where you find me,
And how much longer will I have to lose everything before I remember you, gleaming like an eternal wish at the bottom of my empty well.
How often I have to lose every word but your name before I finally remember how to speak it.
How far into these nights you're willing to follow me . . .

You,
lacing your divine fingers through the dusted fabric of my
flesh and pulling praises up from the ashes of my cries.
You,
orchestrating each swelling second of my life like building
movements in a symphony moving forever closer to
You . . .

This is where you find me . . .
where you've always found me searching, in turn, for you.
Here, with a prayer resounding, sometimes barely whisper-
ing, sometimes only loud enough for you to hear . . .

And what can I say?
With your ear pressed to my heart slammed shut, learning to
open again, what can I say, but that he who has begun a
great work in me will be faithful to
complete it . . .

What can I say
but things have been given
things have been taken away.
Blessed be the name of the Lord . . .
completely.

The life of a follower of Jesus is all about love, for he loves us in
every way. He loves us with perfect *storge,* for we are his children.
He loves us with perfect *philia,* for we are his friends. He loves us
with perfect *eros,* for we are his bride. And he loves us with *agape,*
for he is love.

11

Together

Rebels with Alliances

We work hard with our own hands . . .
when we are persecuted, we endure it;
when we are slandered, we answer kindly.

When we first experience true community, we are exhilarated. People we haven't known before like us. We have all sorts of things in common. We have friendships in abundance. It's kind of like falling in love. But true community begins only when Christians come together long enough to notice each others' faults—and then stay together knowing those faults! It's not that different from the togetherness we experience within a normal family or with close friends when we are committed to them no matter what may come. Even different churches can experience the kinship of Christ if they work together.

Jesus makes people uncomfortable. He made the members of his own family uncomfortable it seems. For a time his mother and brothers thought he was crazy and came to bring him back home. It's much the same way with the young person who comes to Jesus. To be family is to be familiar with one another. We may not be all exactly alike, but we have learned to live with our parents' oddities, our siblings' idiosyncrasies, if for no other reason than we know what to expect. The problem comes when someone within the family unit does something out of the ordinary—in this case something like deciding to become a Christian. Not just a Christian, but a zealous Christian. And not just a zealous Christian, but a young, zealous, stupid Christian who doesn't know when to keep his mouth shut or how to express the new love that is within him.

I became a Christian at age eighteen, straight out of high school. I proceeded to attempt to "evangelize" my family. I was like the proverbial bull in a china shop. I didn't care for their feelings, their hurts or their doubts in comparison to telling them the good news of new life in Jesus. I was, all of a sudden, someone they didn't know. I was *un*familiar. I believed things and was doing things that were outside of their expectations; and as a result, friction came into the relationships we had been accustomed to before my conversion.

I knew that I was still the same person I had been. I was still sloppy about keeping my bedroom in order. I was still forgetful about my household chores. I was still self-centered when it came to my schedule versus theirs. But now I had thrown Jesus in on top of that. I was oblivious to my own hypocrisy. It got so bad at one point that one of my family members said to me, "Mike, if heaven is full of people like you, then I don't want to be there!"

When I realized that I was, by my actions, doing the opposite of my intentions to bring my family closer to Christ, I realized that I needed to start changing. Our togetherness as a family was going to depend upon my actions and not just my words. I have worked at becoming a good brother and son for over three decades and I will never stop.

For those of us who claim Christ, maintaining a community within our own genetic families is a mission that never ends. My brother Mark is two years younger than I am. While growing up we were playmates, competitors and even enemies. I think I was jealous of him; a lot of attention would have come my way had he not been born. This is something every oldest sibling experiences.

As we grew up, he was usually considered better looking by others than I was, and I resented that. He was built differently than I was—stronger and more athletic. I would take advantage of being older and of my larger size to make his life miserable. I remember making him cry and then barricading the door from our bedroom, begging him not to go tell mom and dad. When we would wrestle, I'd put him in a scissor hold with my long legs and squeeze with all my might. (There is a bit of Spartan blood in our family, so he would never give up or let me know how much pain he was really in!)

After I became a Christian, I noticed that things between Mark and me didn't seem to be quite right. (The Holy Spirit has a way of making one aware of reality.) By this time, my brother had also come to Christ. We sat down and had a few long talks about the wounds that I'd inflicted upon him as a child and how they had become a barrier to a healthy relationship. I had not realized how deeply he had been hurt by my actions and words growing up. Then he told me some things I never expected. I had not realized the prominent place I occupied in his life. I had not realized that he looked up to me, as any younger brother looks up to his older brother; so the rebuffs, the disappointments and the cruelties that I inflicted on him were that much worse. I humbled myself and asked his forgiveness. God's grace has flowed within our relationship ever since. My younger brother was one of my very first supporters when we decided to start Scum of the Earth.

It is my conviction that the Christian life was never meant to be lived alone. Jesus chose twelve disciples for a reason. The apostle Paul and the other apostles traveled with a group of several people for a reason. The founders of the church demonstrated that living in community is important. But it seems a large part of the contemporary church thinks differently. There even seems to be a trend among people *not* to be part of an established community of believers.

Sometimes I can understand why. Somewhere in the past, they were inoculated with a dead version of church life which makes them resistant to the real thing when they finally do encounter it. You can go to church on a Sunday, fellowship with the back of someone's head for an hour and then go home, but that isn't community. Sundays for the Christian are a celebration of the life that we have with God and each other the rest of the week. If Sunday church is the only togetherness a person has with the body of Christ, it isn't enough. It's like having dessert without having the meal first. A steady diet of only that every week, and the young Christian is not getting near the nutrition or exercise that is required to be healthy. Instead they become bloated, inactive and judgmental.

I don't think it's possible to communicate the concept of community by mere words. Community must be modeled to be understood. When it comes to Scum of the Earth, all my pleading for people to get into relationship with one another is useless unless I show myself to be in relationship with others. While people from Scum have come into my home, and we've had many meals together, and I go to their homes, and we meet at coffee shops and various places around town, I need community that understands what it's like to be me as well. Specifically, where does a pastor go to get community with other pastors?

There was no senior pastor for a time at Corona where I was on staff before Scum, and so several of us got together and decided to bear the preaching burden as a group. There were four of us, so each of us would preach once a month. We called ourselves the Preaching Team. But that's only half right. It slowly became a men's group, an accountability group and a lifeline. Much to our amazement, when a temporary senior pastor came to our church, he joined the team!

Since that time, the original team members have been scattered to different churches around the city, but we've continued to meet together every Thursday. We go over each others' outlines for upcoming sermons—like a Bible study for each person's passage of Scripture. But it has become much more than that. The relationships that we have formed have kept me from self-destructing several times over the last ten years.

The first half of our weekly meeting centers on our lives: our own relationships, how we are interacting with our spouses and our children, congregations, finances, how we are getting along with Jesus. Then, after we are done with that, we focus on our sermons. I believe in this kind of a meeting so much that I've instituted a preaching team for Scum of the Earth staff as well.

As humans, one of our biggest fears is to be alone. Even prisoners enjoy the company of other prisoners, and one of the worst things that can happen in prison is being placed in solitary confinement. As followers of Jesus, we must have a few friends with whom we can be honest. We are all mixed up—sinners and saints inside of each of our skins. We need each other to celebrate the one and chastise the other.

I will never forget one girl who came to Christ on a night at Scum several years ago. Her name was Jordana. She knew that the first thing the Lord was asking of her, after committing herself to him, was to give up sleeping with her boyfriend. She did so im-

mediately. A couple of weeks after that Jordana found out she was
pregnant. She was too young to raise a child. She was still in
school. She felt like she had no other choice and wasn't strong
enough to go through an adoption. Her intention was to abort
the fetus growing inside her.

Her new friends in Christ came around her and asked her to
reconsider, but she would not. They prayed for her, but she was
still afraid. Then an older woman from Scum shared her story of
feeling rejected by her parents as a teenager. The woman related
the story of Jesus being rejected by all yet continuing to love
people. Jordana knew the people at Scum would not reject her or
betray her if she had this child. Suddenly, the thought went
through Jordana's mind: *I don't want to reject my baby!* That was it.
That night was the first time she had ever had communion—the
bread, the cup. Her communion was with Jesus, to be sure, but
also together with her friends at Scum of the Earth.

The testing of that decision, made because of her friends in
Christ, was yet to come. Through eight more months of pregnancy her friends stuck by her, and together with a pregnancy
center and an adoption agency, Jordana brought the baby full
term into the arms of a childless Christian couple from another
part of the country. Jordana continues to receive updates and pho-
tos and even has occasional visits with her young son.

The body of Christ is made up of many different parts, the
apostle Paul writes in 1 Corinthians 12. Sometimes, in order for
the body to work properly, some of those parts have to work in
opposition to the others. Sometimes I don't like people in the
body of Christ because they are pulling in the opposite direction
that I am. But that doesn't mean they are necessarily wrong for
pulling in that direction.

At Scum, we have difficulty understanding the culture created by suburban megachurches. We're in the city and are fairly

small in number (which I suppose would make us the antithesis of the suburban megachurch). And those are just the beginnings of the differences.

I don't know if there is anything we do that draws as much attention as having homeless people at our services. They eat with us and (if they stay) worship with us. A production crew from *CBS Evening News* came to Scum one Easter for a special presentation on religion. They were amazed and impressed when homeless people and college kids came through and grabbed food, then sat down at tables eating together like it's the most natural thing in the world. You have no idea how difficult it is having homeless people in your church on a regular basis. You get asked for money, some of them smell bad, some of them are drunk, some of them steal things, some of them fall asleep during your sermon and snore really loudly, and some of them will start arguing with you while you're trying to give the message. It's really messy. And the messier it is, the more our people like it. This idea that church has to be seamless and run like some kind of TV show is what the folks at Scum are trying to vomit out of the body of Christ. They're gagging on it.

I remember one time we were having a leadership meeting and people were asking, "Can we *not* use the PowerPoint? Can we just go back to overhead projectors? Or have sheets of paper?" I thought, *You've got to be kidding me! Really? Do we so badly want to distinguish ourselves from the suburban church?* We decided against the sheets of paper because it's eco-friendly to project things electronically. But to have the fancy PowerPoint with the scenes behind the words that move like streams and waterfalls— that would have been tantamount to adding artificial plants to our stage.

What was so funny was that we were meeting at a large church at the time. They had a forest of artificial plants. Our worship

team would arrive early every week to take them all down, until
one Sunday night, they noticed a note tacked to the similarly de-
spised plexiglass drum shield.

> Dear Scum of the Earth: We know that the artificial plants
> are uncool, but they're expensive uncool. Could you please
> be careful when you're moving them around?

Scum of the Earth Church folks and suburban church folks
would not be what I consider "together." That is, until the miracle of 2008.

For a few years we had been looking for a place to call "Scum
Home." The folks from Mile High Ministries had allowed us to
use the Prodigal Coffee House when we first began. John and
Raylene Swanger brought us to The Tollgate for over three years,
and after that, the folks from Church in the City welcomed us
into their building. We were blessed and grateful to have their
love and support—and space! After a while though, you begin to
feel like a guy who has been sleeping on his buddy's couch for
years. One of our staff, Tim Dunbar, sensed a call from God for
us to begin preparing to purchase our own building.

I thought he was nuts. There was no way a congregation that
can't even support its own staff was going to buy a building big
enough to house a few hundred people! But with the skill of an
MBA in accounting (and phenomenal guitar chops), Tim started
to form a building committee to do just that.

Our first building fundraiser was funny, in a way. We had no
idea what building we were going for, so the committee set a table with framed pictures of about ten properties that might work.
People invited their parents, uncles and aunts, family friends,
neighbors, and others. Scum people cooked the meal, served it,
did valet parking and cleaned up afterward. There was a short
program, and we asked for money. Incredibly, we got some! We

also now had a list of people who were sympathetic to our need for a place of our own.

We did this for two years. Before we could plan the third, we found the perfect place. Josh Cook, one of the pastors on staff, was procrastinating writing his sermon when he looked on Craigslist under "church," where he found an old church building that had been converted into a residence and artists' studio. We had never seen it before because it wasn't included under commercial sites. He sent me a link to the realtor's website. We went to look at it with a few people and our own realtor. To a person, each of us said, "This is it!"

We sent a proposal to the sellers saying that we wanted to buy the building. We had no bank financing, but we had the $100,000 we'd raised and a lot of hope in a God who could do anything. We were just about $550,000 short. To our amazement, they accepted the proposal! There was one catch. We had exactly one month to get them the rest of the money, for they planned to auction the building off in thirty days.

That's when the real miracle began to happen.

We called every person who had ever donated anything to our building campaign. We had telethons to every person in our cell phone directories. And we called every church we knew of. The response was overwhelming—especially from suburban churches and their members. By the month's end, we saw the Lord pour $300,000 into Scum's bank account through these friends. That left us a quarter-million dollars short, but God wasn't done blessing us and teaching us a lesson at the same time.

A group of Christian businessmen (from the 'burbs, of course) came to me and said something like, "Mike, we've been watching what God's been doing here for Scum of the Earth, and we want to give you the gift of time. We're going to cash out some of our investments and loan you $250,000 for ninety days. We figure that's about the time you'll need to raise the rest." They wired us the money at closing time. The church building was ours on July 2, 2008!

Three months later, all but $50,000 of what we needed had come into our account in order to pay these visionary businessmen back. We borrowed that amount from a friend of the church, and then paid him back by year's end. "Scum Home" was bought and paid for in just six months.

So, because of the sacrificial generosity of suburban Christians from around Denver, in Colorado, across the United States and overseas, we at Scum can no longer claim any kind of "Christian moral high ground" over our brothers and sisters in the suburbs. Because of their charitable giving and benevolence, we own, outright, a building that we could never have afforded from our Sunday offerings.

One more thing, just to highlight God's economy: we bought the church building at the lowest possible price at precisely the ideal time, right before one of the biggest economic downturns in U.S. history. If those Christian businessmen had left their money in the stock market for those ninety days, they would have lost as much as 40 percent of its value. They got every penny back! I wonder what kind of blessings God has in store for those who *gave* their money away to a bunch of ragamuffins trying to buy a 127-year-old church building. What does God have in store for those young people at Scum and elsewhere who learn the charitable ways of some of those suburban church folks?

I will say it plainly: We need each other. Jesus is God in the flesh, and yet he was born into a family and worked out the difficulties of life together with them. He had at least twelve good friends and scores more people with whom he traveled. And he started a church for us that goes on to this day. Being together is that important.

12

Carried

The Way of Christ

What do you have that you did not receive?

*I*f you go up to the high country of Colorado, even along the highway—especially in the spring—you will see streams that are swollen with snowmelt and moving at a rapid rate. Sometimes you'll see a branch being carried along by the current swiftly down the stream. The branch is not smart enough to navigate the boulders that are in the middle of the stream or the downed logs and trees that are jutting out into its course. But because the water is so high and the current is so strong, the stick is carried either around or above these obstacles, and sometimes even under them.

This picture—a stick in a stream—has been a helpful metaphor for my spiritual life. Often we meander through life or think we know which way to go, but suddenly for a season the force of God's Spirit lifts and carries us in his own direction. It is his great love for us that accomplishes this. It is certainly how I feel about my time at Scum of the Earth Church. I can take very little credit for what has happened there, and yet it has been the most fulfilling part of my vocational life.

In Genesis 12 God tells Abram to leave his country in order to go to the land that the Lord will show him. God doesn't give Abram a map but rather tells him to get up and move. Abram will be directed while he is en route. Many Christians I know want to follow Jesus, but they wait for a definitive word as to where they will end up before they take a step. God does not work that way very often. For some reason, he likes to exert his will upon objects already moving in his direction.

In Acts 16 the apostle Paul and his companions are spreading the word of the Lord. They're making progress in Galatia, but then the Spirit of Jesus does not allow them to preach in Bithynia or into the province of Asia. The Lord finally gives Paul a dream of a Macedonian man asking for help. In obedience to the dream, Paul changes course and heads for northern Greece. Paul was a stick on a stream being carried by a very strong current. God is faithful to direct, redirect and even prevent moving objects from getting stuck in the wrong places.

Believers through the ages have experienced the wonder of being carried by the Holy Spirit. Read about the life of most any saint and you will notice this truth. The weird thing is that often the saints didn't realize they were being carried until afterward. This could have been during times of great success or sorrow, adventure or terror, faith or doubt. A popular parable by Mary Stevenson, "Footprints in the Sand," attests to this truth.

One night I dreamed I was walking along the beach with the Lord. Many scenes from my life flashed across the sky.

In each scene I noticed footprints in the sand. Sometimes there were two sets of footprints, other times there was one only.

This bothered me because I noticed that during the low periods of my life, when I was suffering from anguish, sorrow or defeat, I could see only one set of footprints, so I said to the Lord,

"You promised me Lord, that if I followed you, you would walk with me always. But I have noticed that during the most trying periods of my life there has only been one set of footprints in the sand. Why, when I needed you most, have you not been there for me?"

The Lord replied, "The years when you have seen only one set of footprints, my child, is when I carried you."

I remember, as a small boy, returning from visiting relatives in our family station wagon. Very often I would fall asleep on the way home only to wake up and realize that my dad was carrying me from the car, into the house and up to my bedroom. Those are extremely tender memories for me.

But then I remember getting a bit older. My younger brother was born, and then the twins came after him. Now it was four kids in the station wagon on the way back from Grandma's house late at night. When we pulled into the driveway, I would pretend to be asleep, hoping to be carried into my room. But my parents could carry only the youngest, and so most of the time I was gently nudged and prodded to get up and walk into the house like an adult.

I didn't like that feeling near as much as that of being carried. It could have been worse, I guess. They could have asked me to carry one of the twins, but that might have been dangerous! The faith experience that is reflected in this change, from being carried to making my own way, is characterized in another parable by an unknown author.

One night, I had a wondrous dream;
One set of footprints there was seen,
The footprints of my precious Lord,
But mine were not along the shore.
But then some stranger prints appeared
And I asked the Lord, "What have we here?"
"Those prints are large and round and neat
But, Lord, they are too big for feet."
"My child," He said in somber tones,
"For miles I carried you alone.
I challenged you to walk in faith,
But you refused and made me wait.
You disobeyed, you would not grow,
The walk of faith you would not know.
So I got tired and fed up
And there I dropped you on your butt,
Because in life there comes a time
When one must fight, and one must climb,
When one must rise and take a stand
Or leave some butt prints in the sand.

Granted, the author's viewpoint is a bit blunt. But it's a helpful reminder that for all the talk in the Bible of being carried, we're also regularly instructed to walk on our own.

You yourselves have seen what I did to Egypt, and how I carried you on eagles' wings and brought you to myself. (Ex 19:4)

Walk in all the way that the LORD your God has commanded you, so that you may live and prosper and prolong your days in the land that you will possess. (Deut 5:33)

There you saw how the LORD your God carried you, as a

father carries his son, all the way you went until you reached this place. (Deut 1:31)

Blessed are those who have learned to acclaim you, who walk in the light of your presence, O Lord. (Ps 89:15)

In all their distress he too was distressed,
    and the angel of his presence saved them.
In his love and mercy he redeemed them;
    he lifted them up and carried them
    all the days of old. (Is 63:9)

Whoever claims to live in [God] must walk as Jesus did. (1 Jn 2:6)

For prophecy never had its origin in the will of man, but men spoke from God as they were carried along by the Holy Spirit. (2 Pet 1:21)

Yet you have a few people in Sardis who have not soiled their clothes. They will walk with me, dressed in white, for they are worthy. (Rev 3:4)

So, which is it? Are we borne along by God's Spirit, or do we move on our own? Obviously, the answer is that sometimes we are carried, sometimes we walk on our own, and sometimes we do both.

I find this paradox to be true in people's stories of coming to faith in Jesus. Initially, I hear them speak of their quests to find truth. The late nights spent talking with others about the meaning of life, the hours spent reading various books, the time spent in study of the Bible, the weekends spent in silent retreat, the prayers offered up—these are the marks of someone striving to know. They aren't just walking, they're running to seek ultimate reality. And God rewards their search. He reveals it to them, for

according to Jesus himself, "Everyone who asks, receives. Everyone who seeks, finds. And to everyone who knocks, the door will
be opened" (Lk 11:10 NLT). This is true of my own pilgrimage.
But I see the other side now too.

While I had grown up going to a church, the bulk of whose
service I couldn't understand, I did get Sunday-schooled in Old
Testament stories, New Testament stories and the life of Jesus.
During the Divine Liturgy, my daydreams were informed by the
pictures of saints and archangels, and depictions of the life of Jesus
throughout the church building. I certainly didn't plan for that to
happen. I was immersed in a culture of Christianity—literally,
having been baptized into the Greek Orthodox Church at forty
days old. Of all the places in the history of all the world, God
chose for me to be born into that church community.

At some point in high school, I was asked to be part of a panel
of students who would appear on a local television show hosted by
a prominent pastor in town. I remember him asking each of us
about our belief system. I parroted the things that I had been
taught in church and Sunday school. When the taping for the
show was over one of my best friends, who was also at the taping,
approached me incredulously and said, "Sares, you don't believe
that stuff. I've never heard you talk about it before. Why did you
say that?" The obvious truth of his comments jarred me to the
core. He was right.

In the late 1960s and early 1970s, people were trying out all
types of new philosophies, new religions and new music. In an attempt to keep students interested, my high school English depart-
ment divided its curriculum into mini-courses on contemporary
literature, humanities and the like, but the course that piqued my
interest was called "The Supernatural." In that class we were expected to read books and write papers on any of a variety of myste-
rious practices. I remember doing a project on graphoanalysis (kind

of tame by comparison to the rest of the class) but others were doing projects on séances, Ouija boards, witchcraft and the like.

About the same time that I was taking this class, I met some kids from a Baptist church youth group. I think I might have only gone to one of their meetings, but I became something of a project for them all. In the course of getting to know the kids I also got to know their youth pastor, David Carder. I remember asking David about the parts of the Bible that I was unfamiliar with, and specifically what the Bible says about the end of the world. I was fascinated. I was also a bit humbled that he would take an interest in me. He answered a lot of my questions and even came to my parents' home to talk further.

There is a point in which the person being pursued by any group of religious people begins to feel like a prize at the county fair. While that thought crossed my mind, it was always offset by the genuine affection coming from the group. There was no question that I was being loved in some manner, but that didn't always make it comfortable. I remember one of the more zealous young men cornering me about what I believed on various occasions, even at school. If I saw him coming down the long hallway toward me, I would intentionally avoid him by turning around and taking the longer way to class!

That semester, an idea occurred to me that would combine two of my divergent interests—the occult and Christianity. I got permission from my "supernatural" English teacher to do my next project on the end times, Armageddon and the last days. Part of my project called for Dave Carder to appear in my English class and give his views about the topic. The result was a study in contrasts between Dave and my English teacher. Dave was this energetic, clean-cut young man talking about his faith in God and God's plan for how the world would end, how Jesus would be victorious and how everything would finally be made right. I remember watching him and then looking over at my English teacher. She was a very attractive woman, but the look on her face was one of dislike and displeasure. She was not enjoying this young preacher, nor the topic he was discussing. There was something dark about her mood. I was worried that her mood might affect my grade—and not for the better!

It wasn't until years later that I put the pieces of the puzzle together. I recalled that my English teacher had brought in a good friend of hers, a male witch, to talk to our class at one point. I'd wager that my teacher herself had been involved in the occult at some point, and that was the reason that she designed the mini-course that the other students and I were taking. By bringing in a young preacher of the gospel, I may have unwittingly brought the enemy into her classroom!

Before the end of that school year, Dave asked me if I wanted to accept Jesus Christ as my Lord and Savior. Although I was still not convinced that Jesus was the "only way," I felt that it was something I ought to do. So after visiting his church one Sunday, I knelt down in the back with him and prayed what is known as "the sinner's prayer." I was hoping for a voice from heaven or a lightning bolt—something—but there was nothing. My family moved from that area shortly thereafter and my contact with Dave ended. It wasn't until months later that I would decide to start seeking out answers once and for all. But up to that point, I had been obviously carried.

So there are times we can be carried along like a stick in a stream. There are times we walk as a person on an important journey, but sometimes it feels like both. There's a third metaphor for the Christian life that joins both ideas: swimming. My friend Jim Emig notes that you cannot swim until you relax enough to be carried by the water, but you have to move your arms and legs if you want to go forward.

When problems confront us, the temptation is sometimes to hide and wait for the problems to go away, or to fight like crazy in order to burst through to the other side. This swimming metaphor helps us avoid such extremes. We need to relax enough to see what God is up to, but at the same time, be open to whatever it is he wants us to do. There are changes we can make while experiencing the support of God. It is not one or the other, but both.

When I think back to the times I didn't like what I was doing vocationally—before the move to Denver—I sometimes wonder why Jesus made me wait twelve years after the supernatural, almost audible word at that concert in Michigan. Sure, the prophecy had to do with my involvement with Five Iron Frenzy, and my future ministry at Scum, but it goes so much deeper than that. I think the reason that God spoke twelve years before it actually took place was so I would know that he had not left me during the twelve years in between. All of the self-doubt, all of the financial duress, all of the different jobs, all the seminary classes, all of the wondering if God still cared was not in vain. I had been carried along for a dozen years and was finally in exactly the place where he wanted me to be. I had been swimming the whole time. Finally I was ready to let the current sweep me away.

Being a follower of Jesus is an exercise in this kind of paradox: of treading water, of swimming, or of allowing ourselves to be carried away by the strong current of God's Spirit. It's this sort of exhilarating life that Paul speaks of in 1 Corinthians 4, the passage from which our church gets its name. We become the scum of the earth, the refuse of the world—and that is our glory, for then we are following Christ.

A Scum Benediction

My conscience is clear, but that does not make me innocent. It is the Lord who judges me.

Several years ago, a bunch of young people gathered in our living room and came up with that line in Scum's mission statement: "We strive to be a church that recognizes its need for a savior." I think the reason that people could come up with a line like that was because we all realized that we were broken, that we needed fixing, that we needed a savior, that we were a bunch of sinners, and that we were church people who didn't know how to do church. Where did we come up with an idea like that? It is all over the Scriptures really. Here is one.

> Save me, O God, for the waters have come up to my neck.
> I sink in the miry depths, where there is no foothold. I have
> come into the deep waters; the floods engulf me.
> …
> You know my folly, O God; my guilt is not hidden from
> you.
> …

But I pray to you, O LORD, in the time of your favor; in your
great love, O God, answer me with your sure salvation.
. . .
Scorn has broken my heart and has left me helpless.
(Psalm 69:1, 2, 5, 13, 20)

I'm like the apostle Peter, who found himself on the wave-
broken surface of the water with a thunderously broken sky overhead, crying out to Jesus, "Save me!" as he sunk into the miry
depths. Peter was a guy who knew Jesus, believed in Jesus and
followed Jesus. I'm a guy who knows Jesus, believes in Jesus and
follows Jesus—yet I'm still broken. I still need salvation because I
sink all the time—way too often for a man who's a "professional
Christian"!

It is appropriate that we who love God are needy and that we
need God. A friend of mine used to respond to people who said
that Jesus was just a crutch by saying, "Well, yeah, but at least he
keeps me from falling on my face." I'll take it a step further: Jesus
is my crutch and I still fall on my face. I don't need a crutch; I
need a whole emergency transport system. It is OK to bemoan
this sad truth a little bit, as in the song "House of Broken Dreams"
by the late singer-songwriter Mark Heard.

Hear the whistle blow
It echoes down my soul
It's something I have always known
Nothing sounds so sad
A cry to the unknown
The fundamental sigh of all who've gone this way before
Lay me down to sleep
Come and comfort me
I'll sleep in peace in a house of broken dreams
I'm old enough to know

That dreams are quickly spent
Like a pouring rain on warm cement
Or fingerprints in dust
Nectar on the wind
Save them for tomorrow and tomorrow lets you down again
Lay me down to sleep
Come and comfort me
I'll sleep in peace in a house of broken dreams
Give me the reasons to go on
Soften the sorrow that shatters and bends
And mend broken dreams
Sentimental hearts
Hungry for the past
Penniless at the wishing-well
Memories will last
And cover certain scars
Acquired in the daily grind of being what we are
Lay me down to sleep
Come and comfort me
I'll sleep in peace in a house of broken dreams

I used to sing this song over and over again at some of the lowest points in my life, because I felt exactly like that. I had been a Christian for twenty years, yet my life looked like crap. I had a hard time being a good husband; I had a hard time being a good father; I had a hard time putting bread on the table with a job I had a hard time liking, and somehow, I recognized that I needed a savior. Another "broken" Scripture passage reads,

The sacrifices of God are a broken spirit;
A broken and contrite heart,
O God, you will not despise. (Psalm 51:17)

That is how I feel very often, even today, that I'm, in Mark
Heard's words, a "broken man."

I'm not a loner
No sack-cloth and ashes
Just a heart on a tether with a vagabond mind
But this will be a broken man
Come shivering out of his wintertime
I'm a broken man, a broken man
Outcast on the outskirts of the promised land
A broken man
A broken man
A broken man
I have faltered in my strength
I have wanted to do everything right
I swallow hard while the second hand blinks
Shut the back door to keep out the night
Is it just a game
Is this a maze to lead me right back where I started from
This will be a broken man come shattered from this
    marathon
I'm a broken man, a broken man
Outcast on the outskirts of the promised land
A broken man
A broken man
A broken man
Maybe I fear the crush of guilt
I can't take that kind of weight
Maybe I'm afraid when the thunder breaks
Scared of losing the things I love so much
I pretend I ain't scared
I ain't frightened by no third degree

But this will be a broken man come begging for your
    charity
I'm a broken man, a broken man
Outcast on the outskirts of the promised land
A broken man
A broken man
A broken man

Can you imagine what Mark Heard went through to write those two songs? He was, perhaps, the best Christian songwriter of his time, but most people never heard of him. And he had a hard time providing the bare essentials for his family. Then, still a young man, he had a heart attack on stage at Cornerstone Music Festival, and died a short time later. But he had a Savior whom he sang about as well.

The Christian life is weird and upside down. How strange it is that when I am weak, I am right where God wants me. How upside down that God insists on a mature son or daughter being dependent. The times I have been closest to God are times when I have been literally knocked to my knees. I do not go there willingly to pray, but life just kind of knocks the wind out of me, and I crumple on the floor like someone has just kicked me where it hurts the most. That is when I am closest to God. It is not when I am feeling great, when church is full, or when the offering buckets are overflowing. I am not as close to God when things are going well in my marriage. I am not as close to God when things are going well in my family. I am not as close to God when things are going well with my job or my relationships with my friends and neighbors. The strange thing is that I get closest to God when life is at its worst. Yes, that is a choice on my part, but I look back at the hardest times in my life, and that is where I feel myself closest to God.

As the years go by, those times gleam more and more like gold, and everything else looks like dross because those time are where I learned the biggest lessons that will carry me not just now but into eternity.

The Christian life is strange. The Lord himself says this to the apostle Paul, who is undergoing his own brokenness:

> But [Jesus] said to me, "My grace is sufficient for you, for my power is made perfect in weakness." Therefore I will boast all the more gladly about my weaknesses, so that Christ's power may rest on me. (2 Cor 12:9)

So here we are, stuck in this life where to be broken is really to be the safest, and to be whole is really to be in a dangerous place. Because of this we struggle, we strive, we aim, we try to be a church that recognizes its need for a savior on a daily basis. It is one of the hallmarks of Scum of the Earth.

People come to visit and say, "You're so real." I think we are just telling it like it is. We are being honest. There is nothing really strategic about it. It is not a shtick we do to gain more people or to gain notoriety. It is admitting that we are broken and that we need salvation on a regular basis. We need salvation continually, every day. We are quite in line with Paul's letter to the Philippians:

> Therefore, my dear friends, as you have always obeyed—not only in my presence, but now much more in my absence— continue to work out your salvation with fear and trembling, for it is God who works in you to will and to act according to his good purpose. (Phil 2:12-13)

We are continuously converted. I repeat: we are continuously converted. We are always broken, so therefore we are continuously converted.

It is as though my body is this house full of rooms, and when I asked Jesus into my life, I gave him the key to the front door. It was great for him to stay in the foyer for quite a long time, until he wanted to start knocking on the other doors in the house—like the bedrooms. It took me a while to want to let him into those rooms. But if I didn't open the doors to let him in, he kicked them down. After that there were closets that really contained dark things that I didn't want Jesus seeing, but there again, he was bent on continuously converting me. I was going to recognize my need for a savior whether I thought I needed him or not. It will go that way until the day that I die and I finally have all my doors flung wide open (the windows too).

So we have a problem: we see ourselves as better than we really are. We've done this since we were children. I think the hallmark of being childish and immature is that you think you are better than you are. When I was eighteen and nineteen years old, a new Christian, I was God's gift to the church and the world. I was intelligent; I was mature for my age; I had a good sense of morality; I was energetic; I got a lot of stuff done; and I had so many talents I didn't know what to do with them.

The problem with thinking like that is when you think you're a small sinner, like I was at eighteen and nineteen years old, all you need is a small savior . . . and if you're a tiny sinner, you don't need a savior at all, because you can handle it all by yourself. We read the Scriptures; we go to church; we listen to the sermons; we read the books. We know in our heads that Jesus will save us, but our hearts disagree. We know enough to know that we need Jesus in our lives somewhere, somehow, at least for eternity's sake, but we don't really know that we need a savior after we become Christians.

Isn't that odd? It is like we have been turned into these little tiny Pharisees without even trying. Randy Stonehill sang about it in his song "That's Why We Don't Love God."

Although our lips feign praise, still our hearts are far away.
That's why, that's why we don't love God.
We're so consumed with self, we can't love anybody else
We mask the nakedness of our mortality cloaked in this
        poison pride and the illusion of control.
We need the gift of grace more than the air we breathe.
But as it draws us near, still it repels our stubborn souls
That's why, that's why we don't love God
Oh yes, our lips feign praise; but our hearts are far away.
That's why, that's why we don't love God
I don't want my prayers to be some meaningless litany.
Why are we so afraid, guarded and counterfeit?
Is it because we know all the shadows we conceal?
And we are so alone—wolves in the winter snow—
Never imagining that this mercy could be real.
We say we need a little help.
We need some new direction.
Avoid the blessing like a curse.
We're only lying to ourselves.
What we need is resurrection.
What we need is second birth.

There is something crazy about Jesus; he draws us in with promises of eternal life and wholeness, but the closer we get, the more we are repulsed by the truth that we are broken, that we are needy, and that we desperately need a savior. That is why we don't love God.

There is a solution and the solution is this: we need a real picture of ourselves as broken people who recognize our ongoing, continual need of a savior.

Now, we are always looking for saviors. I know this because I know myself and because I talk to people at Scum of the Earth and other churches—and while, in your head, you're thinking "Jesus is my Savior and I need him because I am broken," in your heart, what you are actually saying is, "If I could only get a boyfriend, then I wouldn't be broken anymore. Then I would have my savior."

"If I could only find a girlfriend."

"If I could only get married."

"If I could only get my spouse to understand."

"If I could only move to a new town."

"If I could only go to school."

"If I could only go to a different school."

"If I could only get a new job."

"If someone could only help me get out of debt."

"If I could only . . ."

Our hearts are full of longings for other saviors than the One that we have because we refuse to see ourselves as broken people in need of a savior.

The beauty of the gospel is found in our brokenness if it leads to a genuine redefinition of our relationship with God. Once we can admit to ourselves that we are totally messed up, we have a totally new relationship with Jesus.

One of the things that I appreciate about Scum is that it is the kind of place where I can come and be real and honest about what is going on in my life. Now, naturally there are degrees of honesty that come with levels of friendship. I am not going to say in front of everyone on a Sunday night what I would say in a staff meeting, but I can assure you that we routinely share our brokenness at staff meetings. Right now I am going through a terribly sorrowful time. It has to do with my family. I question what kind of father I've been. I question what I could have done differently. I question whether or not, had I been a better husband, things would have turned out differently for my children. It has not all been nice at my house with me as husband and father. I share my own physical problems with the staff because, though some of the problems are embarrassing, these are the people that I walk with. These are the people that I trust, that I hope trust me. If I cannot share my decrepitness with them, whom am I going to share it with?

The qualification to be in the church is to realize we are not qualified to be in church. I often tell people to stop looking for the perfect church if you are out there shopping around—because if you join it, you will wreck it! Better to throw your lot in with a bunch of people who know they are screwed up. I have perceived myself as a failure financially for more years than are proper. I feel like I have always been struggling to make ends meet. I have had electricity turned off at my house. I have had the water almost turned off. I have had to accept groceries from churches. I have had to stand in the unemployment line. I have had problems at my house that I cannot afford to fix for months at a time. This is not something to be proud of; I'm in my fifties! This is the kind of thing that should be history. I should have had enough money in the bank to go and call a plumber and have him fix it. I didn't. Why not? Because I made stupid choices.

I have failed as a pastor and leader. Sometimes I wonder, "God, why? I am not smart enough to do this job. You have to help me. You have to let me know what the next turn in the road is because you know I don't have a five-year plan. I barely have a two-month plan." I tell him, "Lord, I am so undisciplined, why would you pick someone like me?" I don't know how people at Scum should feel about this, having such a slacker for a pastor. If I were them, I would be embarrassed.

So what can we do? We can mourn our brokenness. Jesus said, "Blessed are those who mourn, for they will be comforted" (Mt 5:4). He is saying, "Happy are you when you're sad—because then I can comfort you."

What do we mourn? We mourn the status quo. I do not care who you are; you could have the greatest life around. You could have plenty of money in the bank. You could have the greatest relationships on earth. You could have the job that is from heaven. But there are little girls in Thailand who are being sold into prostitution at the age of seven, and if that doesn't cause you to mourn, I don't know what will. There are people in India who are not being given the basic rights of human beings because they were born into the wrong family. That should cause you to mourn. There are people in the Sudan who are being killed because they are Christians, and that should cause you to mourn. There is the porn on your computer or the shoes that you paid way too much for. Then there is the realization that we, as the richest people in the history of the earth, have caused others—the poor—to suffer just by consuming more of the world's resources than we ought to.

So you see, there is always something to mourn in the status quo. How long has it been since you have faced the depth of your own sin and brokenness? I ask that question because we can avoid it pretty easily. If that is so hard for you to face, then ask this question of yourself for the next week: "Why is that hard for me to face?" That question can then lead into, "What has God saved me from, and what does he want to save me from in the future?" and "What are the problems I've had in my life that he's actually mended, but where there's more work to do? Where is there still brokenness?"

Needing a savior is a continual thing. We need to examine ourselves on a daily basis and ask ourselves what we can expect from God. I think he wants us to expect something every day. He wants us to be dependent.

I can't think of a better way to recognize our need for a savior than to partake of Communion, the Lord's Supper, the Eucharist, on a regular basis. It is there that we recognize that we are messed up. That we are broken. It is there that Jesus says, "Come freely and eat. This is my body; this is my blood, given for you that you may have new life in me." The people who need to watch out are the people who come to eat and drink thinking that everything is fine, that they don't really need a savior, that they are not broken. In their heads they may have the right words, but in their hearts they are far, far away. Those are the people who need to watch out.

If you, however, come to Jesus broken and looking for mercy and looking for grace, then you will drink the cup the way Jesus meant it to be drunk, and you will eat the bread the way Jesus meant for it to be eaten. He gives himself to us because we are broken. Let us always remember that we, every one of us, are the scum of the earth—a church worldwide that desperately recognizes its need for a savior.

LIKEWISE. *Go and do.*

A man comes across an ancient enemy, beaten and left for dead. He lifts the wounded man onto the back of a donkey and takes him to an inn to tend to the man's recovery. Jesus tells this story and instructs those who are listening to "go and do likewise."

Likewise books explore a compassionate, active faith lived out in real time. When we're skeptical about the status quo, Likewise books challenge us to create culture responsibly. When we're confused about who we are and what we're supposed to be doing, Likewise books help us listen for God's voice. When we're discouraged by the troubled world we've inherited, Likewise books encourage us to hold onto hope.

In this life we will face challenges that demand our response. Likewise books face those challenges with us so we can act on faith.

likewisebooks.com